POLKA PUNCTURES

A JOURNEY THROUGH THE HOWS, WHYS, HIGHS AND LOWS OF RIDING A BIKE

Rob Whittle

Polka Dot Books

All rights reserved. No part of this publication may be reproduced, stored in a retrieval system, or transmitted in any form or by any means, electronic, photocopying or otherwise, without the prior permission of the copyright owner. This is not a training manual, and anything written herein is, although based on fact, merely opinion.

©Rob Whittle 2020
©Polka Dot Books 2020

Paperback ISBN 978-1-8382862-1-7
Ebook ISBN 978-1-8382862-0-0

Cover Design: Rob Whittle

ALL RIGHTS RESERVED

CONTENTS

INTRODUCTION..................................1
PROLOGUE......................................4
1. WHY?..12
2. THE BIKE....................................20
3. THE BIKE FIT...............................29
4. KIT..30
5. CYCLING COMPUTERS....................48
6. INDOOR TRAINING........................54
7. OUTDOOR TRAINING.....................64
8. RIDING UP HILLS..........................67
9. RIDING DOWN HILLS!....................80
10. CADENCE AND GEARS..................87
11. WEATHER..................................93
12. ON-BIKE NUTRITION...................109
13. TO STOP OR NOT TO STOP..........112
14. WEIGHT....................................115
15. SPORTIVES................................127
16. THE HOLIDAY PROBLEM...............142
17. ACCIDENTS................................148

18. CRAMP………………………………160
19. MECHANICAL!……………………164
20. TO SHAVE OR NOT TO SHAVE…….171
21. HOW TO AVOID SQUIRRELS……….176
22. HOW TO AVOID MOTORISTS……….178
23. ETIQUETTE……………………………188
24. PARTNERS……………………………..195
25. WATCHING CYCLING…………………201
26. DO YOU HAVE TO STOP PEDALLING WHEN YOU FART?…………..209
27. AGAIN, WHY?……………………………211
ACKNOWLEDGEMENTS…………………226

INTRODUCTION

"Ride as much or as little, or as long or as short as you feel. But ride." Eddy Merckx

In "Polka Dots and Punctures", I look to address many of the issues surrounding the present-day act of riding a bike around. From the somewhat mind-boggling plethora of bikes to choose from to the issues we cyclists might have with our fellow road users and to why we would want to ride at all. We'll take in such subjects as the weather, hills, and fitness along the way, and may even find an answer to the single most important question in cycling: do you have to stop pedalling when you fart? It's aimed at those of you who have just started out on this potholed strewn road, but I hope that more seasoned cyclists will also see their own experiences mirrored here.
I have, along the way, formulated twenty-five laws that constitute a Cycling Theory of Relativity. These are constants that hold true for my two-wheeled experience. They're not in any particular order of importance – I wrote them as they came to me – although Law 1 could be said to be the most basic and fundamental to this thing we call cycling.

Cycling is now a hugely popular pastime. And it's not surprising, because riding around on two wheels can be great fun, can be great exercise, and can be great for the mind. Like many, I returned to cycling having simply forgotten its joys. One day, I put the bike away and I didn't get it out again for another twenty-five years or so. Upon my return, there were so many changes: what I knew as 'a racer' was now 'a road bike', for a start!

To new cyclists, or to those who, like me, returned after a long break, there is a bewildering amount of choice and information out there. I've been riding my bike around for a while now, and I've managed to pick up a bit of knowledge and experience along the way, stuff that I wish I'd known when I was just starting out. It's my hope that it could be useful to others and so I've cobbled it together into some sort of book. Some of it's based on science, some of it not, and most of it's based on my cycling life (so far) and plain old common sense. There's also a fair bit of autobiography and anecdote. It's definitely not in any way a training manual, rather a collection of my own opinions. There will be parts many might agree with and, equally, sections many do not, but, since there's no definitive 'right' or 'wrong' way to ride a bike, I might just get away with this!

Pretty much everyone can ride a bike (except my mum – she never quite got there) and, to some, cycling can be variously a mode of transport, a pastime, an exercise routine, a sport, or a complete way of life. I love riding a bike, so much so that my wife, Shelly, recently pointed out that cycling's all I bloody well think about, to which I of course replied:

"What's your take on disc brakes?"

Shelly is generally happy that I cycle. However, she does despair about how much of my life it has taken over. She's right when she says it's pretty much all I think about and, when I'm not riding, I'm looking at routes, or bikes, or books about bikes, or watching other people ride on the telly. She's happy that I'm very fit and healthy for a guy my age but worries about me out on the road. I point out that I'm doing it all for her and she should think herself very lucky to have a husband with the body of a racing snake and a positive mental attitude.
I also tell her that, while she is (well, we are) paying her gym memberships, cycling is free!

Obviously, it is, once you've bought the bike and kit. And then upgraded.

Polka dots and punctures represent the highs and lows of cycling for me, from majestically cresting a mountain to sitting by the side of the road with oily hands and a wet backside. Obviously, there are lower lows (not many), but "Polka Dots, A Broken Collarbone and A Twelve Week Layoff" doesn't quite have the same ring to it. So, there you are.

Hope you enjoy the ride,

Cheers,
Polka Dot Rob Whittle
("The Flying Goat of Leafy Cheshire")

PROLOGUE

Like most, I remember the first time I learnt to ride without stabilisers. For me, it wasn't a moment in the park with Dad running along behind, a joyous tear in his eye, shouting "I've got you!" when, really, he didn't. The truth, as it mostly is, is far more mundane: I taught myself by riding round and around in circles in the back yard until, at one magic point, I no longer had to put a foot down.

That was on a tiny, blue Raleigh with white wheels, which I had inherited from my older brother. Being a second son meant that most material things came to me through him (although, on the plus-side, he had to have the tap end of the bath). So much so that I awaited his birthday as eagerly as my own because I got to see what I would be owning a couple of years down the line. Dad was not one for unduly splashing out on new things, which meant that, as we grew, we didn't necessarily see shiny, new bikes, just shiny, new bits of the seat post. We all knew that it was new bike time when it got to that point where there was so little post left in the seat tube that it began to wobble. The problem was that Dad never raised the handlebars, the result being that, with backside high in the air and head well below it, we resembled an aero racer, well ahead of their time. That, or just someone extremely interested in what was going on with their front tyre.

Riding a bike gave me a freedom to explore. First, around the block and then, throughout the whole estate. More importantly, it meant I could tag along with my brother and his mate (who, as the younger sibling to a girl was, unfortunately, staring down the barrel of a brown Raleigh Twenty… complete with shopping basket).

When my brother got, on his eleventh birthday, a racer – they weren't called road bikes back then – a silver Sun GT, I took on the green Puch that had been bought for him because Dad felt that a Raleigh Chopper was inherently dangerous to ride: an odd decision considering the way he set up our bikes. This stayed with me for four years until, at last, I obtained my first brand new bike! It was a Raleigh Arena GTX, and I went absolutely everywhere on it: well, to school and back, or to my mates' houses and back, or to the park and back, where it normally served as a goalpost. When I outgrew that, I didn't wait for Dad, I just took on my brother's Carlton Continental, that he had already bought second-hand.

1984 (or it might have been 1985 – whenever it was, apartments were still flats and continental quilts had yet to become duvets.) Summer holidays and, with nothing better to do, me and my friend Tommo decided to go for a bike ride. The planning of such excursion was not in any way what you would term 'comprehensive', we simply decided one day that the next day we would go on a bike ride. Luckily, it turned out to be a warm, sunny morning when I turned up at his house (although, strictly speaking, his parents owned it) on my Raleigh Arena GTX, so the trip was most definitely ON. (Unlike today, we would not have ridden anywhere, apart from school, in the rain, so any hint of precipitation and we'd most probably have stayed in and watched The Young Ones videos or listened to Tommo's records.) I can't recall the make of his bike but what I do remember is that we'd spent a day or two earlier in the month sanding down and repainting the bikes with Hammerite. His was black and mine sky blue. It was a slightly 'different' look we were going for.

We were dressed how we always dressed to ride our bikes: tight jeans, t-shirts – his was probably a Joy Division one, mine New Order – and trainers. Actually, I had made one concession to our forthcoming athletic endeavour and was wearing tracksuit bottoms. They were maroon Manchester City ones.

Although I was/am a United fan, Auntie Anne washed the kits at City and so I tended to get the odd cast off. I would never wear a jersey, of course, but shorts and trackies were fine. Her husband, George, was such a strong City fan that he wouldn't let us have United on in the house – our house – when he came round. He was an excellent artist, forever bedecked in double denim and the tattoos he got in the Navy. They lived in a tiny terraced house, dark and full of paintings, a stone's throw from Maine Road.

It never struck us that there was such a thing as cycling gear. The sports shop sold stuff for, football, cricket, rugby and tennis, badminton or squash, but that was about it. Even the bike shop only sold bikes and bits of bikes (and, oddly, model railways). We'd never seen anyone on the road wearing lycra and the only time we'd ever seen somebody remotely close to our own age wearing proper cycling kit was on the Yellow Pages advert on the telly: "Look at that saddle – be like sitting on a razor blade! Maybe next year, eh?"

Even when Kevin Keegan fell off his bike on 1970s sports/entertainment show, "Superstars" (which was probably the only time I would watch competitive cycling on the television), rather than proper cycling kit he was wearing a vest and disturbingly short shorts, garments we wouldn't be seen dead in outside of the school gym (or even inside – he looked like he'd forgotten his kit and had to use the lost property bin).

To us, 'cycling gear' was just whatever gear we were wearing at the time with a bike stuck between our legs.

Neither of us had bottle cages so, appropriately, neither of us had bottles. We both had pumps under our top tubes, though, and Tommo had a Swiss Army knife, just in case of emergencies. After a couple of pieces of toast and a coffee each, we rolled out of his drive and left Timperley, south of Manchester, heading east, suitably unprepared and armed only with the aforementioned pumps and knife, plus an old Ordnance Survey map and a few quid in our pockets. From my house in Oldfield Brow to Tommo's in Timperley it was a mainly flat –

perhaps ever-so-slightly downhill – couple of miles, and this was about as far as I had ever been on a single trip. (I had to check this on Google Maps and was surprised as I remembered it being at least twice as far. I upped this distance by a long way when I found a local fishing venue, 'local' being ten miles away. 'A long way' back then constitutes a warm down ride today.)

Everywhere else in my life at that time was contained within that radius: all my other pals, school, park etc. I don't recall what we thought we were letting ourselves in for, but I know we were pretty optimistic. I suppose the thinking was that, if we could easily ride two miles, we could easily ride ten, and, if we could easily ride ten miles then twenty shouldn't be a problem, and so on. It's the kind of sunny outlook that explains why we didn't think we'd need any food or drink.

The first few miles were easy, although we did miss a turn at one point and get slightly lost embarrassingly soon after we'd started, but we conferred with the map and it wasn't long before we were back on track, and found ourselves riding on the A6 heading out of busy Stockport and into the countryside towards Buxton.

Until now, 'riding up hills' for us had meant short rises of no more than a couple of hundred yards, and certainly nothing approaching half a mile. Even the toughest hill I knew (Bonville Road, just up from my house) steep though it was, was only about a hundred yards long, if that. There had always been respite available after a minute or so. Suddenly, we were thrown into a world of pain on a road that appeared to be going up for ever!

If only I'd noticed all those contour lines on the map. Fortunately, it levelled out a bit when we reached Disley.

There were, of course, many short descents along the way but, all too soon it seemed, the inclines began once again as we passed though the small towns of Whaley Bridge and Chapel-en-le-Frith, crawling slowly along main roads towards our goal. Eventually, wonderfully, we crested a rise and saw Buxton nestled in a hollow below us. We freewheeled into town and stopped at a shop on the hill that dropped into the centre to get some refreshments. For me, it was a Lion bar and a can of Lilt, and Tommo had a Mars and a Pepsi. It's amazing to think now that, on a ride on a hot day, that lasted somewhere between sixty and seventy miles, this is all we had to keep us going. We rode down into town where we turned west, past the Opera House, to head home.

As we cycled out of Buxton, I spotted lorries dragging themselves slowly up the side of a hill. I looked at the map. I looked at the hill again. And looked at the map. Bugger, we were going up there.

Already tired from our thirty or so mile outward journey, we now had a mountain (well, a big hill) to climb, so we put our bikes into their smallest gears and set off up the slope that led to the Cat and Fiddle pub. Although my bike had started out life with ten gears, it had, through my own mismanagement, become a five speed. Consequently, my smallest gear was something like 52x24 (a ratio I would not like to have to push up a steep hill anytime soon – I'm more than happy with the 34x28 I use these days).

I lasted a couple of hundred yards before I was off and walking. Tommo got a bit further, but then became transfixed by the cats' eyes in the middle of the road and decided that he wanted one. He promptly sat down on the tarmac and tried to dig it out with his Army knife. These days, I don't think he'd have lived too long after planting his backside down – back then, there was far less traffic about, but, even so, he was unable to dig his prize out, and we were soon on our way upwards again.

All told, it took us a little over an hour to ride/walk the three miles up. At one point, we thought we'd made it as we reached a brow where the road tipped downwards, but there was no pub to mark the top! We crested this rise only to find that the pub was still a distance away, across a wide, shallow trough – seemingly so close that we could almost touch it. Like a mirage in the desert, it was a trick of the eye and we still had a mile to go. Although we could afford to freewheel for a while, we soon had an arduous drag up to the final and definite summit. We were well and truly knackered and could (and should) have stopped at the pub for a bit of refreshment. We didn't, though, because we were more than eager to ride down the other side.

Apart from slow moving or stationary traffic, I'd never actually overtaken a car before and here we were, flying past motors of all shapes and sizes. Tommo led the way down and I followed his line, getting by cars and lorries as swiftly as possible so as not to lose his tail. At one point, he caught a curb on a turn with his left pedal and had to virtually run along with his bike to stay upright, but we carried on going, laughing at how close he'd come to grief. It was so exhilarating, riding the wide twists and turns as fast as we could pedal (and faster) before the road dropped through a wood and arrowed down to the end in Macclesfield. To ride those seven miles down, it had taken us less than a third of the time that it took us to ride the three miles up.

The last part of the ride, from Macclesfield to home, was a bit of a grind. There was a lumpy road to Alderley Edge, briefly highlighted by the speedy drop down to the village, and then a long drag back home past the airport, probably made tougher than it should have been by a lack of fuel.

We'd been out most of the day but, because we were both home in time for tea, no-one missed us. Once back at school, we regaled friends with stories of our epic journey, but nobody was the remotest bit interested.

Oddly, as much as we had enjoyed it, we never did plan another ride like that one.

1. WHY?

Why ride a bike?
It's a simple question, isn't it?
Many of us who'd ridden around as children never questioned this. It was just a natural progression from first learning to walk upright and then learning to run. Bikes were freedom – a magic way to get further faster – and that was that.

But then we grow up, and bikes aren't always the way we want to project our teenage image. Oddly, at about the time that I was beginning to prefer beer and four-wheeled transport (not at the same time), I fell in love with the sport of cycling. I say, 'fell in love', but it was just a summer fling: three weeks every July (highlights on Channel 4).

Over the next few years, it remained this way. I was a keen fly-fisherman and still did plenty of sport – football, squash, golf even – but I rarely got on my bike. While I was discovering that the professionals didn't just sit around for the other forty-nine weeks, and that there were different races in other countries - the Giro d'Italia and Vuelta a Espana, and then all the one-day races – my bike was busy gathering dust in the cellar. I began to develop this love for the sport of riding a bike a long time before I returned to doing it myself.

My reacquaintance with two wheels came about because it was just something to do to help a mate. He was doing a sportive for charity and asked if I would train with him as it had been years since he'd been on a bike. When I dusted the cobwebs off the old Carlton Continental back in 2009, I had no idea that it would lead me to where I am now, especially when I was completely shattered after our first foray on two wheels, which was something slightly less than ten miles. We gradually upped the distances over the summer, and I was enjoying it so much I felt the need to purchase a better bike. (You might find that this can be a recurring need.) My steel Carlton with the wibbly-wobbly wheels returned to the cellar to be replaced by an aluminium Boardman which had, to my amazement, gear levers in the brakes! It took me a good few weeks to stop reaching for the downtube to shift up or down.

By the time it came around, I was cheerfully confident that our charity ride would be a doddle: so much so that I shot off like a rocket. After only five miles, I bonked spectacularly and crawled round the remaining 45 miles in a state of bewilderment, grinding to an almost (but not quite) complete halt every time the road even suggested it might go up. I eventually dragged myself in an hour behind my friend, who was standing at the finish, waiting, equally bewildered as to where I'd been all this time. It was the hardest hell I'd ever put myself through. He no longer rides his bike. He carried on for a bit, but then conspired to ride into a parked van and break his collarbone. I think it never had quite the same appeal for him after that.

I can't get enough of it. Go figure... The reason I carried on after the disaster that was that first sportive was because I'd done so badly in it. I wanted to go back and get it right. I guess it's a stubbornness I have, a part of my personality that goes hand in hand with the fact that I am never wrong. Looking back, I was riding my bike relatively little compared to now – about 800km that year, mainly restricted to Sunday mornings – but, when I returned to do the same ride the following year, I had still put in enough work and improved to be able to knock an hour and a half off my previous time. It helped that I had paced myself. I set myself a target three hours for the fifty miles and so had to do an average of 17 mph, something I managed to keep to. I never stopped eating and drinking all the way around. It still wasn't easy, of course. When I finished, my back hurt, my arse hurt, I was covered in snot and my hands and bars were horribly sticky from gels and drink, but I came in at 2 hours 58 minutes and I was ridiculously happy.

By now, I'd decided what kind of rider I wanted to be. Watching those Tours years before, it was all about the mountains for me. I saw myself as the goat, dancing on the pedals: a climber, a grimpeur. I didn't quite have the physique, but I had the will and, importantly, a polka dot jersey! Even then, there was no sense of 'training' as such, although I was, simply by riding the bike. I dropped some weight, which was nice but, again, this wasn't a motivator for me. I went out most Sunday mornings, either with mates or alone, but rides were never really much further than 40km. Still, the more I rode, the fitter I got, which made these rides – especially the group ones – less of a grind and more of a treat.

Cycling just seemed to fit me so well. The single biggest factor when I got back into it was simply that that I really enjoyed riding a bike and rediscovering that sense of adventure I'd not had since I was a kid. Add to that the fact that I like to push myself and that it's very much an individual thing: the only times I did actually go on my own mini bike trips as a kid were when friends were absent (holidays, shopping with mums, avoiding me like the plague etc) and I was forced to make my own fun. Even then, cycling for cycling's sake was a wholly individual event. (I suppose I do not like to have to rely on anybody else.)

Even when out riding with my pals, it was me against the road and me against my head. As much as someone could try to help if I was in a spot of trouble, pacing me and keeping me out of the wind, still, it was me against the road and me against my head. It's this kind of struggle that motivated me, and is probably the reason even now that I find it hard to go on an easy ride.
Added to all this, was the fact that I wanted to be a mountain goat, so I better bloody well start finding some mountains to turn myself into one!

This was the start.

The Theory of Cycling Relativity:
Law 1
You get out of cycling what you put in.

January 2016

I'm in the garage and sitting on the Boardman, which is now my turbo training bike. It's sub-zero, but I'm just wearing my bib shorts, a T-shirt, and cycling shoes. A towel hangs over the handlebars. My breath pushes misty clouds towards the laptop screen while I wait for the DVD to load. The turbo, an Elite RealTour, came packed with workouts, one of them being a Mont Ventoux program, mimicking the slopes involved. I'm hoping the 'virtual ride' that arrived in this morning's post will make the experience all the more real, and have rigged up a portable tv to help with the illusion. I haven't put the garage's fluorescent tubes on (the flickering bugs me) so the two screens are the only light in the otherwise pitch-black darkness. Eventually, the DVD whirs into action and I am presented with moving pictures of the road that leaves Bédoin: wonderful! It's accompanied by Europop: not so wonderful!

I start the Elite program in sync with the DVD and off we go. Two things are apparent right from the start. Firstly, the film has been taken from the roof of a car, giving me an unnaturally high viewpoint and, secondly, we are going quite fast. I double-check the box to see that the length of the film is only sixty minutes. Yes, I think, we'll be zipping up the mountain quite quickly.

It doesn't take long to warm up, and, ten minutes in, more steam is rising from my back than being blown out of my mouth. The drips of sweat have begun to form my turbo puddle beneath me.

Because the video has had to be dropped back from the car's initial filming speed, but is still going way too fast, I find myself flying past slow-motion cyclists. Saint-Estéve is long behind me and I am flying through the forest by the time the Elite's program has me reaching that famous bend. Abruptly, it puts the brakes on, and my happy spinning slows to a more measured grind. I'm still holding at about 200 watts, but my cadence has dropped from 95 to 80. I'm now too hot for the T-shirt and so sit up to take that off, taking great care not to bring down the two sets of step ladders that are hanging right above my head. The sweaty T-shirt gets thrown to the side and I notice it get caught and hang neatly on the vice I got from dad's garage when he died. A brief memory pang: that, his hand drill, beautifully made and powered by cogs, and the red oil can that never seemed to be empty and lubricated all my chains as a kid.

Back to work, and the song has changed for the umpteenth time but it's still the same beat. It doesn't really matter – I'm now only listening to the sound of my own breathing. Tapping out the cadence.

We're suddenly out of the trees and at Chalet Reynard, where we veer left and up. There's a fleeting image of a wonderful view and I want to see more, but the camera, fixed and emotionless, swings round to follow the road. I can now see the mast at the top! I glance at the RealTour program on the laptop to see that I am lagging well behind, but, because it's a pretty steady gradient, it doesn't matter too much. I just

keep tapping out my 80 rpm and holding that same power.
Three more songs bang out and I've passed Tom's monument, flown up the final kilometre, hairpinned right and arrived at the top. On the tv screen, I've just done twenty-one kilometres. On the laptop, I'm just approaching thirteen. I briefly consider carrying on to complete the computer program, but an hour's enough, isn't it? I climb off the bike, turn off the electrics, grab my sodden towel and T-shirt and go indoors. I reckon, based on that, the real thing should take me just under two hours.
Better keep up the training.

2. THE BIKE

The bike is somewhat essential to the cyclist. Without one, you are merely a jogger, in the same way that a snail without a shell is just a slug. (This is, perhaps, why joggers always seem a bit, well, grim.) You can have all the other gear and spend hours at home dressed like a cyclist but, without the bike, you're just wasting your time. Trust me, for this to work, you need a bike.

Bike prices can range from the marginally expensive right up to the "f*** me! I could buy a car for that!" so, if you haven't already got a bike, you have a great deal of homework to do.

1. What type of riding do you want to do?
Yes, there are different types! You have road riding, for which you might want a road bike (obviously), but you will also find commuter bikes, single speeds, hybrids (not the petrol/electric kinds), and e-bikes (which are electrically powered, but there's still a fair bit of pedalling involved). There's off-road, so we have mountain and cyclo-cross bikes. And, more recently, there are gravel bikes, which are a sort of a cross between road and cross – a do-it-all, if you will.

Of course, they're not so specific that there can be no crossover, so you could use a mountain bike on the road, or take a hybrid up a dirt track, but they are what they are because, like all good tools, they fit the job best. If you are looking to buy just one bike, it's probably best if you decide how and where you want to ride first.

2. Say you want to be a roadie.
All of these bikes will have their own subspecies so, for example, road bikes come in slightly differently shaped frames, depending upon whether you want to be sat low down and spread out or in an easier, upright position (generally referred to as race and endurance geometry), and they will come in different materials, which tends to have an effect on...

3. Budget.
These days, road bike frames can be made from carbon fibre, aluminium, steel or titanium. Each material has its strengths and weaknesses, and each comes at a different cost. Generally, aluminium is cheapest. It was The New Thing back in the 1980s, when it looked to be the replacement for steel. Since then, it has itself been superseded by carbon. Most pros these days ride carbon frames. You'd therefore come to a quick and easy conclusion but, things are never so simple, and it does not necessarily mean that one is better than the other.

If you do want a carbon frame, then they tend to come in different types, and this can be one area where two seemingly identical bikes can vary widely in price. A higher modulus carbon comes at a price. The frame may be stiffer and lighter than that made from a slightly lower grade material, but you'll have to decide whether these aspects are worth the extra cost.

The bits that attach to the frame will vary in cost, too. Probably the two most important things to look at are the wheels and the groupsets. Bike bit manufacturer Shimano, for example, presently has four levels of mechanical and two electric groupsets – which is basically the gears and stuff. (Other companies, Campagnolo and Sram, also have their own versions.) Each comes with its own price tag. The difference? Weight, as always, is an important factor, and the slickness of shifting (moving from one gear to another). These days, due to the ongoing technical arms race between the three companies, a new groupset seems to come out every other year, relegating the old one to a lower level. This trickle down means that even the more basic gearing is still pretty good. Good enough that, like the carbon frame, you would have to ask whether the marginal gains are worth the somewhat hefty price difference.

Similarly, wheels can be light, or they can be aerodynamic, they can be a bit of both or, most depressingly, a bit of neither. Because the bikes you are looking at are likely to come complete, it is important to look at the package. With a complete bike, it is common, in order to hold a certain price point (say £2000), that a great frame can be fitted with lower quality groupset, wheels, etc. Conversely, a slightly cheaper frame can be made up with better kit. Sometimes, but not often, you get the best of both worlds. It is also true that you might pay a premium for a more well-known brand. This does not necessarily make it a better bike and you might well find that you get a much better package from what might be seen as a lesser name. If you have a budget to stick to, it is vital that you DO YOUR HOMEWORK because:

The Theory of Cycling Relativity:
Law 2
Sometimes, the better bike is the less expensive one.

Happily, the resurgence of cycling has meant that competition in the market is strong. Bike manufacturers cannot really afford to make a dud. For someone just setting out on the road to cycling happiness, lower specification kit on less expensive bikes should not really be an issue and, actually, the difference between a £1,000 bike and a £5,000 one will not be as discernible as you might imagine. There are many, many very good bikes at that cheaper price point. Going back to frame material, for the same money, you could get a very well-equipped aluminium bike that might be a far better buy than a carbon-framed one with somewhat cheaper components. If you simply have to have carbon, it might be well worth planning a little for the future. The great thing is, because a bike is a sum of its parts, it can be made better by changing the parts! You can do this by concentrating on finding a great frame for the money, and then upgrading the parts down the line. It is also worth noting that there are many outlets that will happily allow you to tweak before you buy.

And then spend weeks deciding whether you want rim or disc brakes.

4. N+1

Having gone through all this - having budgeted; researched; tried before you buyed (bought doesn't rhyme); and finally come to a decision; wavered, because it's a lot of money; finally come to a decision again and made a purchase – you now have a shiny new bike. This is your pride and joy, and you are emotionally torn because you want to go out and ride it, but you do not want to get it dirty. Your partner may be equally torn: you've spent the price of a holiday on something that doesn't even have an engine, but they've never seen you so happy.

Do not be surprised, though, if, by the following day, you are perusing cycling articles looking at bikes again. This is the rule of N+1, where N is the number of bikes you own. It now does not matter how many bikes you have; you will always feel that you need another one.

My first purchase upon my return was a Boardman Comp. It turned out to be a good bike for the £600 it cost, although I was left reeling from the price: the last time I had been involved in a bike buy, I watched my dad get the guy in the bike shop to take £21 off the price because there was no way he was paying over a hundred quid for a bike! To be fair, nearly thirty years had now passed. The Boardman was aluminium-framed and had a mixture of slightly lower-grade, but still problem-free, components. I rode it happily for four years before I got the itch and upgraded to a carbon Focus Cayo Evo WITH ELECTRONIC GEARS!!! I had some great times on that but, after another four or so years, I started yearning again, and much time was taken up trawling magazines and web pages.

Even when you've done all the research and have a pretty good idea of what you want, sometimes you just can't get it. Here is my experience whilst mulling over whether to treat myself to a new bike:

"YOU CAN HAVE ANYTHING YOU WANT, AS LONG AS IT'S BRIGHT YELLOW."

I honestly hadn't thought it would be a difficult request to fulfil. I had been looking to get a new bike, seen the one I wanted, and I wanted it in a particular spec and colour. But: problem.

Because each spec was colour specific, even though the frame was exactly the same, I could not get the spec I wanted in the colour I wanted. I thought I might be mistaken until I mentioned my quandary to a well-known brand's representative

"That's right." he said.

"But all the frames are the same, aren't they?"

"Yes, that's right. Different groupsets, wheels and what have you, but all the frames are the same."

"So, what happens if I want the bog-standard, mechanical Dura-Ace bike? I have to have it in bright yellow?"

"Yep."

"Even though it's exactly the same frame as the much nicer silver Ultegra Di2 build?"

"Yep."
"Why? Why, if it's the same frame, can't I pick the colour I want and then have it specced accordingly?"
"Because then we'd be making far too many frames in far too many colours. We couldn't do that!"
I was beginning to think that I was part of some bike version of the Monty Python "Cheese Shop Sketch" when I thought I saw light at the end of the tunnel.
"We do sell the frameset on its own, in silver." the rep offered, "We could get one and build the bike up for you."
"Great! At the same price?"
"Oh, no. That would probably work out quite a bit more expensive."
"For the same bike?"
"Ah," he said, "but in a different colour."
I walked away, thinking about runny Camembert and cats.

The thing is that bikes these days can cost a lot of money. An average spend is probably not far off the three and a half grand I was considering forking out. For that amount of money, no matter how good the thing is, no matter how much lighter, or faster, or more comfortable it is, I do not want to have to think: yeah, but could I live with that colour? I do not want to have to make that compromise. I'm all for different colours (although I'd be quite happy with boring black myself), but it has become apparent that the wide choice available is not always as it seems.

Consumer is king, or so I thought. I suppose that the manufacturers will only take note when, at the end of a year, they still have a shed load of bikes in their...shed. Certainly, I have yet to see that brand's bright yellow bike out on the road. Much as I buy my kit to match, it should be that the bike follows suit. I don't want to have to consider respraying a brand-new bike to fit my personal colour scheme in the same way as I would not think to add clothing as an extra outlay if I buy a new steed.

I've played this game before. When I bought the Focus Cayo Evo, I'd gone to get an Izalco Pro, but the new year's model was blue (everyone had sold out of the previous year's black incarnation) and I did not want a blue bike. The Cayo was black, white and red, which are my colours – every bit of kit I have is one, one of the others, or a mixture. It was also the previous year's model, almost identical to its younger sibling and, since I knew:

The Theory of Cycling Relativity: Law 3
Next year's bikes always come out this year, which make this year's bikes last year's, and last year's bikes are always cheaper.

I knew I would get a bargain.

Shelly tells me that I wouldn't mind what colour car we had, and this is true, but I don't see a car in the same way as I see my bike, which is an extension of me. A car is just a thing: a bike just isn't. (And, when your dad used to drive you around in a brown Austin Princess with a black vinyl roof, you're pretty much happy with anything.)

3. THE BIKE FIT

It has struck me more than once that, in all my years growing up, I never had a bike that was bought to fit me. Even the first one that was specifically for me, rather than a brother's cast off, was bought (much like that first school blazer) with my future growth in mind and would have been, as I wheeled it out of the shop, far too big for me. Riding the Carlton today, which served me for years as a teenager, I still feel that I am a shade on the small size for it, so heaven knows how I rode it comfortably back then.

I never had a bike to fit, but I never had any problems. Whether it was because my younger self was more flexible, or that the riding position was more relaxed, it just was not an issue.

Time, alas, does not always heal, and my more recent self has had three bike fits and numerous instances of Merckxian tinkering* to get me to a position where I can have a fully pain-free cycle.

My view is that it is pointless forking out a couple of grand for the pleasure of being in pain every time you ride your shiny new bike. Every time you get a bike, get a bike fit.

Next.

[*Eddy was almost as famous for his constant bike adjustments as he was for his amazing win record. He would even start tweaking his saddle in the middle of a race, having spent much time beforehand getting it just right.]

4. KIT

With kit, as with the bike, the most important thing is fit. You're going to be wearing this stuff, possibly for hours at a time and probably during some of the more physically taxing moments in your life – the last thing you want to be worrying about is restricted reach, cold and wet hands, or sore genitalia. The temptation when you're just starting out is to skimp on this bit, but you'll only have to replace everything once you've learned the hard way. You don't have to spend hundreds of pounds for good stuff (although you very easily can) so, like with the bike, do your research.

SHORTS: Shorts and tights are most important as they will hold the main bits of you that are contacting the bike (unless you're wearing them wrong). Look for a snug fit and a good quality protective pad. Take great care putting them on – I've seen them worn both back to front and inside out, though, sadly, not at the same time. If you stick to black, they will go with all your jerseys.

JERSEY: Jerseys are short-sleeved. Jerseys are long-sleeved. Jerseys are relaxed fit or aero. Jerseys are summer cooling. Jerseys are now water resistant, so you don't need a jacket. Jerseys are plain, or colourful, or retro! Again, fit is key, and then go for whatever style you fancy, even if it's replica team kit. If you feel good wearing it, you'll be happy on the bike. It's always good to have a short-sleeved and a long-sleeved base layer, too – that way you're covered for most occasions.

JACKET: Recent jersey tech has made the jacket less essential than it used to be but it's still a good idea to have one for when the weather is really crap, as jerseys will likely hold back the elements for only so long. Remember: water 'resistant' is not water 'proof' - you'll stay much drier with the latter.

GILET: It's like a coat, but with no arms!!! Good for rides that start off cold but then the weather warms up, or for long descents when the wind is likely to cut through and chill you. The lack of sleeves means the gilet takes up less room in a pocket when stowed (so, room for another banana).

HELMET: Opinions on helmet effectiveness are split, with many feeling that wearing one encourages a rider to take risks they wouldn't if they were lid free. Doctors have also cited that much damage is also caused by the percussiveness involved in a fall - that the problem is the brain sloshing about inside the skull - which is something a helmet cannot protect against. Some just want to feel the wind in their hair.
My view is that if there's a way of putting a protective layer between my head and the tarmac, I'm for it. (I ought to wear one around the house, such is my propensity to find cupboard

doors, low ceiling rafters or toilet seats (it happened) with my head.) I don't have any hair.

SUNGLASSES: I cannot recall one single incident when I used to ride around as a kid (which was pretty much all the time) when I got any sort of insect in my eye. Now, if I leave the house for a ride without my sunglasses, I have an optic guest before I've managed to get twenty yards! How does this happen, especially when there are obviously fewer numbers swarming about these days than there were forty years ago? It is greatly perplexing. Glasses also protect your eyes from the sun, wind, rain, and all the crap that splashes up from the guy in front on a wet ride. As much as they are functional, they can be a fashion item, but beware, if you make the wrong choice, you might end up looking like a dick.

GLOVES: A good pair of fingerless mitts helps cushion the hands against road vibration and adds extra palm protection if you come off and, for colder days, you can use fully fingered versions. All this sounds simple, but winter gloves, in my opinion, are perhaps the most difficult item of kit to buy. Hands can really suffer on cold rides and so you need to get it right, but gloves can turn out to be too bulky, too thin, not warm enough, too warm, not waterproof when they're supposed to be, difficult to get on and off. You'll usually find that it takes much trial and error before you find the perfect pair, and then they'll be discontinued.

SHOES: Expensive, light and stiff means nothing if they're not comfortable. Enough said.

BAR TAPE: Okay, so it's not technically 'kit' but there's an important decision to be made in terms of colour. Cycling, even on the best of days, can be a sweaty, grubby business. Any colour other than black will very quickly show this. As The Beatles said, get black.

On top of all this there's socks, arm and leg warmers, overshoes, caps, buffs etc. The list can be pretty long and everything on it, at one time or another, will turn out to be essential (usually when you don't have it).

"IN DEFENCE OF TEAM KIT"
Out on a ride one morning, I was called a 'Team Kit Wanker'. Waiting at a roundabout, another cyclist came alongside and clocked my Lotto Belisol jersey. I said "Morning" and he replied with the three words and left me to watch his Rapha-clad backside ride away as I stood stunned and digested the slight.
It had happened before, although not so overtly, during the Tour of the Peak sportive, which takes place mainly around the hillier bits of Derbyshire. Whilst I had stopped halfway up the Cat and Fiddle climb to take off a couple of layers, a group of riders shot by downhill with a shout of "F**k me, it's Andre Greipel!" Maybe they were going too fast to make an accurate comparison, as I liked to think I was more of a Tiesj Benoot

shape and, even then, there were some marked differences. He invariably has matching shorts, team bike, youth, power, speed, talent, and a gratuitous J. And he was not likely to be seen ploughing a sweaty furrow around assorted parts of Cheshire and Derbyshire of a Sunday morning. However, I understood that I was being laughed at for daring to wear a pro team jersey. And I wasn't even in full team kit. So, this brings up two questions: why do the likes of me wear pro team kit, and why is doing so frowned upon by other sections of the cycling fraternity?

For my own part, all my kit has to be variations of red, white and black – my bike livery – so , amongst my tops, the three replica jerseys I own are a Tour polka dot jersey, a retro Molteni one (black), and that Lotto jersey. Even the club I ride with rides in black and red.

The only one I had an explicit reason for buying was the first. As I said in an earlier chapter, since watching Channel 4's coverage of Le Tour in the mid-80s, the King of the Mountains was the rider I wanted to be. Even during my 20-odd year hiatus from actually riding my bike, I thought that, if I did throw a leg over a saddle again, it was a certainty that this would be my niche. When I returned to cycling, images of Chiappucci and Virenque (great role models both!) flying up Alps flooded back, and it was one of the first bits of kit I bought. I didn't know then that I might be crossing some sort of line by doing so. I wasn't aware of unwritten rules. I just loved the jersey.

I've read pros old and young saying that, by wearing iconic jerseys, we lower forms of cycling life are in some way besmirching them. I'll be honest, I don't attach such importance to clothes but, while I don't ever consciously believe I am in some way honouring the jersey, there is absolutely no bloody way I am going to put a foot down riding up a hill whilst wearing the polka dots. I'm not saying I would never stop if I absolutely needed to, but it certainly helps with my mindset.

In the minefield that is the TKW issue, where does 'classic retro' sit?

The Lotto Belisol jersey I bought as I saw it as an immediate modern classic, very much along the lines of the old Flandria kit and the black Molteni jersey is a new take on an old classic. Obviously, the latter has strong Merckx connotations, but I am well aware that he was a slightly better cyclist than me and, by wearing it, I am not attempting to honour, compare myself, or even summon up the spirit of Eddy: I simply like the jersey.

So, how old does a replica jersey have to be before it can take on the mantle of 'retro'? At the time of writing, the aforementioned Lotto Belisol top is now coming up to four years old and has been superseded three times since I bought it. The nature of pro cycling teams means that they will not only change kit but also names, so Lotto Belisol are now Lotto Soudal. Team Jumbo-Visma are the latest incarnation of the famous Rabobank squad who, themselves, began life as Kwantum in the mid-80s. Do you have to go back as far as Rabobank to be considered classic or retro, or is it okay to stop at, say, Belkin? In the same way, wearing the latest Movistar jersey might be taboo, but it appears to be perfectly fine to don Reynolds or Banesto.

Contrast this with football fans, who turn up in their thousands to watch the teams, dressed in team jerseys, some, even, with the players' names and numbers on the back. (The only ones who routinely get called "wanker" are the guys on the pitch.) Importantly, everybody has to have their own team: you can't just like the game for the game's sake. It seems plausible to me that this aspect of fandom was brought in to cycling in the UK during and after the 2012 boom in interest in the sport. It was an interest that was on the rise throughout the early Noughties but, with a hugely successful Olympics and Tour de France, cycling suddenly found itself thrust into popular culture, and every fortysomething wanted to be a Wiggins. Because most of the new fans were used to the football way of following a sport, you had to have a team to support and you had to show it explicitly: the roads were suddenly full of Sky kits and Pinarellos.

The problem was that many of these converts were either new to the world of cycling or had not been on a bike in quite some time, and so could not properly ride the bikes they were on (or, sometimes, fit into the kit they were wearing). They were not used to the speeds and handling of modern bikes, they had no basic road sense and did not know "The Rules", a list of dos and don'ts for the would-be cyclist. The long-time club riders viewed them as dangerous interlopers on their roads and the pro team kit was seen as colours of ineptitude: "All the gear and no idea".

Interestingly, I believe that wearing team colours is not so much of a taboo on the Continent, and cycling fans there are no less partisan. Perhaps it is – like our attitude to drinking, or eating certain animals – a peculiarly British thing.

For myself, I have no team affinities. This is one of the reasons I love watching cycling as much as riding the bike itself. That I wear a Lotto Belisol jersey doesn't mean I want one of the boys in red to win. I was thrilled with Teisj's Strade Bianche victory, but that was more about the conditions during the race and the way it unfolded than any personal support.

Plus, it's not so easy to identify with a team when the team's identity can transform year on year: it's tricky to nail your colours to a mast when the colours have a habit of changing. Pro cycling is a sport where a rider can change sides simply by staying put.

Occasionally, Shelly will ask me who my favourite rider is, and I cannot provide her with an answer. I love that I have the freedom to enjoy the spectacle without being tied to anyone. Sometimes, I can't help myself – you always want a great rider to go out on a high, so Tom Boonen's or Fabian Cancellara's final Paris-Roubaixs* are prime examples – but, generally, I'm happy to sit on the fence and watch the race unfold. If I do nail my colours to any one rider, it is because of the way they have ridden rather than who they are. This is why I see no problem in wearing team kit. It means nothing to me other than the fact that it is just something to wear whilst riding my bike that looks pretty good. And, if I look pretty good (which I do), I feel pretty good. So, I say to anyone, if you want to wear team kit, bloody well do so and sod the snipers! Unless it's Castorama.

[*Roubaixs? I've never really had to think about pluralising this. It looks wrong, but I'm sticking with it.]

"WHITTLE'S STIFF SHOE THEORY"

I've often read that cycling shoes should be three things: stiff, light, and comfortable - much like the bike. As such, like the bike, shoes tend to come in at three price points depending upon sole material. Cheaper shoes have nylon composite soles, then we move up to fibreglass, and the most expensive (stiffest/lightest) are carbon fibre.

My own first shoes were nylon soled. My current pair are carbon.

The main selling point is the stiffness, to such an extent that we now have a 'Stiffness Index', which goes up to 10. Or 12 or 13 depending on who you ask. The notion is that stiffness equals efficiency, which would seem obvious. But is it?

Whilst riding along, mulling over the possible purchase of a new pair of shoes, I started thinking about what was going on down at the end of my legs. I reckon I have a pretty good pedal stroke – it's something that I work on from time to time – but I've noticed that, for most of the stroke, my heel is not actually in contact with the inner sole or, if it is, it is so very lightly indeed.

This is backed up when watching pro races on the telly. On the run-in to the finish, you can see riders tightening their shoes. The inference of this is, of course, that they had been riding all but 5km of a stage of perhaps 170km with loose shoes. Loose shoes are probably more comfortable, but they are not as efficient. They are certainly not as stiff as snuggly fitting, properly tightened shoes.

We do not put power down equally across the foot when pedalling. This is because pedalling is not unlike running on tip-toes. Our feet are attached to the pedal under the ball of the sole, and so everything happens there. Very little, if any, power goes through further back in the foot. If I do try to push down equally with my heel, it would actually work against the stroke. In fact, I have to I lift off the heel so that I can put power down through the ball. Ah, but what about the idea of "scraping dirt off my shoe" at the bottom of the stroke to eliminate a power dead spot? I would use my heel there, wouldn't I? Well, yes, but I am actually pulling the foot back against the upper rather than putting power downwards.

And then, once at the top of the stroke, I put power down and forward again, but, once more, with the ball of the foot.

So, because we use the ball of the foot to transfer power to the pedal, this is where the cleat sits. Because we have a cleat, we have a reinforced interface between foot and pedal (something that would be missing should you be wearing trainers on flat pedals). We now have this reinforced interface where power transfer happens, so it does not matter how stiff the shoe sole is. There are three layers, one on top of the other: this is how plywood works!

A fully stiff sole would only be needed if the cleat-pedal interface was under the centre of the foot. In this scenario, without a fully stiff sole, you would apply power equally across the foot but the natural arch in the sole would want to give around the pedal, the sole would flex, and thus efficiency would be lost. However, we don't pedal like this.

I had then thought that perhaps the idea of a super-stiff sole was to eradicate numbness or hot spots which can blight riders, particularly on longer rides. It appeared to me that a stiff sole would help dissipate the constant and centralised pressure that would come from the immovable cleat-pedal interface. This notion was knocked back when I saw an advertisement-article on a Shimano training shoe (a shoe specifically for use on your indoor trainer!) where the Shimano spokesman stated that they specifically went for a more flexible sole "to help mitigate isolated fatigue in the foot".

So, it seems to me that, rather than stiffness, the major factor in cycling shoes should be overall comfort, and that a happier foot will actually be more efficient than a totally rigid one. Certainly, my first shoes, the cheaper nylon ones (£60), were just as, if not more, comfortable than the subsequent two pairs of carbon-soled shoes I have had since (about £300 combined).

I hasten to add here that there is absolutely no scientific basis for this theory other than my own common sense (which, itself, is highly questionable) and the only testing I have done is riding around a bit, looking down, and muttering "Hmmm." This is why I have named the theory after myself and why I probably will not be bothering the Nobel jury anytime soon.

EARPHONES?

I can't wear earphones on the bike. I see riders with wires coming out of their ears – or, now, just those little plastic bits, such is the wonder of wireless technology - and think "What are you doing?" And it's not just cyclists – it's runners and rowers, too. It seems that, for many, exercise and music walk, ride, run and row hand in hand.

But I don't get it. Even when indoor training, if I do have any music other than what the training app du jour is offering to help me through the pain, it's played out to fill the room, much, sometimes, to Shelly's chagrin. I can't completely cloak myself in the sound.

One time I did try earphones, I was on the rollers and the static created by my exertions caused the headphones to release electric charges to my ears every couple of seconds or so. A wonderful example of some sort of physics at work and, as Pavlovian exercises go, it was quite effective: that was that for the headphones.

For me, I like to be wholly in the environment. If I'm out in the countryside, I need to hear the countryside. The experience should be sounds as well as sights. (I've no real sense of smell, so I have to make the best of those other two senses.) I don't wish to be accompanied by The Stone Roses – much as I love them – and I don't require Stephen Fry's melodious tones transporting me away to a fictional world.

I don't want to be taken away from anything.

What I need is to hear, over the wind in my ears, the birds singing above and in the hedgerows; or the dogs barking as I pass; motorists shouting "Wanker!" – stuff like that. Just that sound, even when there is no other, of being outside. It sounds corny but I suppose it is 'being at one with nature'.

Riding is often a social thing. I guess I spend half the time riding solo and the other half riding with mates. They have told me of a guy they used to ride with who would routinely turn up to group rides with earphones in. It was a pretty bizarre situation because, should he decide to speak, he would have to do so by shouting over whatever he was listening to. He then could not hear any replies. He did not, I am told, last long in that group.

It's a funny thing because I do have my 'head songs' – the stuff that will pop into my brain and join me on hard climbs, particularly if I'm riding alone. They are songs that sit happily with the cadence I am tapping out. Along with my others, "My Sharona" is so successful at being an earworm it will join me everywhere, if I'm not careful. It is now stuck in my head writing this. It's stuck in yours now, too, isn't it?

Why would I want to impose a soundtrack on an activity that does not need one? I cycle, on one level, to get away from things like that. The phone's with me, but only for emergencies. I may take the odd photo but only if I've already stopped: to eat or stroke a horse (you have to stop to stroke horses, or, at the very least, make that 'click-click' noise as you go past).

The Garmin's there as well, but I'll only look at that once I'm home and hosed, and the heart rate strap, useful though it might be, has never left the house. I need to be unfettered by such things.

So, when I see another rider on the road plugged in, I can't understand why. Isn't simply being there music enough? I can't understand why someone would wish to be in any way taken away from the act of cycling. It's not just the outside noises. It's the sound of your own breathing getting heavier and heavier going up that hill, or your heartbeat in your ears throbbing ever more quickly as the going gets harder. Why drown that out? Listening to your body is part of the process.

Even my head songs fade to nothing as the road continues to tip upward, to be replaced by my own body's soundtrack. This is partly because I can no longer keep to their cadence but also because when I'm really working, everything else just slips away to be replaced by the sound of my heartbeat.

If I was listening to The Stones, Dire Straits, New Order or, unlikely as it might be, the latest John Grisham, I'm not sure I could zone out like this, particularly because, unless you're listening to Elgar whilst riding around the Malvern hills or "Windmills of Amsterdam" on a loop whilst riding around The Netherlands, the sounds in your ears are so totally at odds with what you are seeing. Music has its place, but I don't want it joining me around the lanes of Leafy Cheshire or up and over the Cat and Fiddle into Peaky Derbyshire, not least because I need all my faculties about me when sharing the roads with the 4x4s of the former and the gravel wagons of the latter.

Let's face it, cycling is a pretty risky pastime so cocooning yourself in sound is just adding more risk, to you and to other road users. It's far more important to hear the sound of that car coming up behind you than Kylie's greatest hits.

But let's get back to my main point. The psychological freeing that cycling outdoors offers is lost within the constraints of earphones. Earphones are insular and constrict the world to the self, rather than opening it up. Wearers likely do so for motivation or concentration. This can be great for training, especially indoors, where the music offers some sort of distraction for what can be boring drills, but it kills the magic of riding outside.

ALL THE OTHER STUFF: To go on my bike, I devoted a great deal of time looking for suitably feathery bottle cages. I was understandably very happy when I found some carbon cages at only 28g each. (I could have gone lighter, but would have spent more than I wanted.)

Recently, I picked up my jersey, which still had in its pockets all the paraphernalia I tend to take with me on a ride (take note: a summer ride, so no raincoat here), and was a little taken aback by the weight. It got me thinking – I'd spent all this time worrying about bottle cages only to load the bike in different areas - and so I put everything that isn't fixed on the bike already, that I routinely take with me, on the scales.

This included:

Bottles 500ml x 2, full of water; saddlebag, small, with one tube and two tyre levers; multitool; extra tube, for emergencies; mini pump; phone and keys. (No gels, fig rolls or bananas were weighed, and I didn't include the computer as I forgot and I'm not doing it again, because it took nearly a minute out of my life.) The weight of all this? 1.7 kilos!

Water, obviously, was the biggest offender – one litre weighs one kilo – but that's a pretty essential bit of luggage.

It's a lot, though, isn't it, 1.7 kilos? Especially if you want to be a bit of a weight weeny.

July 3rd 2016

France is bloody gorgeous, isn't it? We've just left the A7 south of Montélimar and are making our way south east into the Vaucluse region and towards our holiday accommodation. It's been a long and increasingly hot drive under a clear, azure sky down from last night's stopover just outside Lille. It's uncomfortably hot, but I'd rather it be uncomfortably hot and sunny than, well, any other alternative. We didn't come all this way for rain.

We are still miles away and, already I've seen it. It wasn't unexpected. I'd read that it stands alone and can be easily viewed from fifty and more miles away, but, still, it's a bit of a shock. I have to stop the car and get out. What a huge bastard!

"What a huge bastard!" I say.

"You can't climb that! Are you sure you're going to climb that?" asks Shelly.

"I'll be alright." I reply, basking in her confidence. "All the roads are up the other side. The 'shallow' side." I joke, now slightly ruing my decision to ride up it three times in one day to join Le Club des Cingles.

I get back in the car and Shelly takes a photo: she wants to remember the look on my face. We drive onward. The mountain keeps getting bigger. By the time we've taken our final turn and are winding our way up the Toulourenc valley on the D40, there isn't much to see out of my window other than mountain. I've got the window open and I have to stick my head out at an odd angle if I want to find sky. We trundle through St

Léger-du-Ventoux, pass a road which shoots steeply off and up to the left to a place called Brantes, and then, in another mile or so, we turn right, over a bridge, to arrive at the sleepy hamlet of Savoillan (one church, one boulangerie, one small restaurant, a few houses), our base for the next two weeks.

Literally, across the road from our house is Mont Ventoux!

Well, that should be a nice daily reminder.

5. CYCLING COMPUTERS

In a world where we now spend most of our time looking at a small screen it would be unfair if cyclists were left out. The cycling computer is a nifty little piece of tech that can give you any data from time, speed and distance to heart rate and power, with or without navigation. Essentially, it's a training tool but, as we are always training – an easy ride is 'recovery', isn't it? – we always need it.

Like any bit of tech, the general rule is that the more you spend, the more you are likely to get BUT this only follows if you can be bothered to read the instructions. There's no point forking out a couple of hundred quid on a unit if you're only interested in seeing how far and how fast you have been going, even if it is the best on the market. The flipside of this, of course, is the same as with buying any bit of kit: always remember that, within a day of buying it, you'll be looking to upgrade.

Computers don't do it all alone just yet, so they have to link to other bits and bobs that you can stick on your bike and yourself – cadence sensors, power meters, heart rate monitors etc – to give you as a complete a readout of a ride or training session as you could want.

As Karl Pearson (1857-1936) said, at some point between those dates, "That which is measured improves. That which is measured and reported improves exponentially". At about the same time,

Lord Kelvin (1824-1907: he who came up with the best, ultimate and never to be beaten zero) came out with, "If you can not measure it, you can not improve it." I suspect Kelvin said it first, but it's known as Pearson's Law, so Karl must have had more Twitter followers. Neither were cyclists of any note.

We generally want these metrics because we want to see that we're getting better. The downside, of course, is that our computer will just as happily deliver the crushing news that we're not.

And, in this ever-shrinking world of social media, it's a given that there's a place that we can see just how well/badly we are doing compared to everybody else.

STRAVA

1969 is a great time in human history: man walked upon the surface of the moon, Merckx won absolutely everything at the Tour, and I was born. (These three events aren't linked...as far as I'm aware.) In the very same month as that final, obviously most momentous happening, Marvin Gaye and Tammi Terrell sang "The world is just a great big onion". These days, it seems, that the world is just a great big segment, such is the popularity of the social fitness network that is Strava.

If it ain't on Strava, it didn't happen!

It's odd to think of all those miles I rode as a kid that are now lost in the mists of time. These days, even a short trip to the shops would be logged. And, these days, it's also kilometres.

The Theory of Cycling Relativity: Law 4
One mile (for those of a certain age) = about eight and a half kilometres.

Strava is the logical next step to having a computer. You do a ride, you have all this data (more or less, depending upon the unit), so what do you do with it? It began, I believe, with three friends who were split by a continent but still wanted to share their rides. It has become, amongst other things, a worldwide site for competition. How you use it is up to you.

I think that the competition can be healthy, but an undue focus on Strava can take the focus off the ride. A few years ago, I spent a little time riding once a week in the evenings with a local group. On my first ride, we were barrelling along nicely and holding a brisk but still reasonably comfortable speed when, suddenly and without notice, they all shot off, leaving me with my bottle in my hand and a somewhat confused (I assume – I couldn't see me, but that's what I was going for) look upon my face. Eventually, after riding hard on my own for about two miles, I managed to catch up to them.

My opening question, once I'd caught my breath, boiled down to, "WTF??? What was all that about?""

"Segment." came the reply in unison.

I tried to make sure that I always had my wits about me from then on but when, a few months later, I was castigated by one of the group for not holding the wheel during another 'segment surprise', I made that my last ride with them. Far too serious for me.

And that's the thing about Strava: everywhere is a segment! And not just one, as Strava is positively schizophrenic when it comes to bits of road. The unassuming 2km stretch just around the corner from my house is six segments, all with their own names. My ride up the single road from Bédoin to the top of Mt. Ventoux* took in, at the time of writing this, a bewildering 156 segments (including "Bédoin to Ventoux", obviously). That is, remember, just one road. If I'd have known I was up against all that, I might not even have started.

There is probably a segment or three up our stairs and there's a very good chance that neither I nor Shelly hold the KOM.

[* I'll probably mention this ride a lot. Not only is it the best morning I've ever had on a bike, it's a great example of many things.]

I have found that the best way to use Strava is to not be remotely bothered by what anybody else is doing. Of course, it could be said that this is the great motivation, but you'll likely be up against younger, fitter riders, some of whom will have trained for and targeted a climb or segment and even, possibly, driven to it to save all their energy for when they got there. It's no surprise then, that when you rock up, having ridden thirty miles into a headwind to get there, your valiant crawl is nowhere near bothering the hallowed leaderboard.

Rather than putting yourself up against those you've never met, use Strava as a personal tool. If you want to compete, compete against yourself. My few places higher up in the rankings have only come because I was pitting me against me, and trying to beat my own times. (Given that I am "The Flying Goat of Leafy Cheshire: Scourge of All Inclines", I am up against one of the all-time greats and have my work cut out every time I sling my leg over a top tube, but this has not stopped me!) Of course, it's hard not to get caught up in the moment of competition, especially if you get a notification that you've actually done well on a segment, but I still see it in terms of lowering my own time, rather than beating somebody else (even though the outcome will be the same). Segments can go up, they can be along the flat, but they do go down, too, and I see an inherent danger in pushing oneself to the limit on a descent just to get a place on a leaderboard with people who, for the most part, you will never meet. As I've always been a big map fan, I find Strava an interesting tool to browse to work out routes, climbs to ride and, perhaps, ones to avoid. It's nice to know how many miles you've ridden and how steep those hills were, although accumulating miles is not the be-all and end-all to riding a bike and, if you're looking for fitness, might not always be the best way to go about it.

And don't be put off by the fact that Dave X holds all the local KOMs and regularly gets far more kudoses (kudoes? kudi?) on his ten-minute morning commute than you do on a hundred miler with 4,000m of climbing. As with Facebook and Instagram, there will always be annoying bastards like that.

[Strava Admission: During the 2020 Coronavirus outbreak, restrictions meant that I had to greatly shorten my rides to an hour which meant that, for the most part, I stayed within a radius of about five miles from home. This meant that, although I love my local lanes of Leafy Cheshire, I began to tire of the same old routes, and I ended up needing something to break the rides up a bit: to make them more interesting. So, I admit it, I did go out to specifically target a place on the leaderboard of a few segments. I found it quite addictive and would upload my ride as soon as I got home in the hope of seeing those little gold medals and trophies. I managed rather well but I still don't hold the KOM up our stairs.]

6. INDOOR TRAINING

Indoor sessions are a great way to keep up fitness, either on rollers or on a turbo trainer. I'll be honest, I used to scoff at indoor training, believing the miles you did on the trainer didn't count. I was wrong, mainly because it turns out that, unlike riding on the road, there are no free miles indoors. If you stop pedalling, you stop. It's depressingly like being a jogger.

To a lone cyclist in a household, setting up for indoor training can prove to be slightly tricky as you'll need to find room to put your trainer and bike. "How much room could I need?" you ask. Well, ideally - but not essentially - this will include a mat (for sweat – believe me, there will be some!), a fan, a computer (laptop, pad, or even phone), and also, but not essentially, a television (the bigger the screen the better). So, as you can see, it's very easy to spread out and become an instant problem to cohabitees. You could set up in a garage or shed but it's much nicer to be inside. Even then, it is highly likely that you will be banished from the lounge relatively quickly.

My trainer is set up in the spare bedroom. We got rid of the bed to accommodate it. Should we have guests… well, they'd better not scratch the bike.

Once you are set up, wherever it is, it is commonly known as a 'pain cave'. The reasons for this become obvious pretty quickly, as we'll see a little later.

Choice of trainer is quite important since there are certain things rollers bring that static turbo trainers do not, and vice versa. Rollers are great for bike-handling skills. Their 'rolly' nature means that, initially, it's like riding on ice and it will take you a little while to master. Start with something next to you to hold onto – a wall, door frame, sturdy chair, grandparent in surprisingly good condition – until you get going and be aware that it will be as precarious to end the session as it was to begin. For this reason, as a novice, do not clip in until you've ridden a few times. If you've hit the tarmac at a junction by not unclipping in time, this is similar, only you are a few inches higher up and always within striking distance of an irreplaceable heirloom. Even once you do get reasonably proficient, never forget that you are constantly at the mercy of balance and gravity. I once came to grief when on the rollers whilst watching Manchester United on the tv: the ball came over from a corner and I instinctively rose to meet it. As Solskjaer hit the back of the net I hit the deck.

Basically, rollers consist of three drums that rotate beneath your wheels, two under the rear wheel and the other up front. There are units on the market that can change resistance, but the classic types are totally free flowing. You stay up, as you do out on the road, by pedalling and the magic of physics, gyroscopic effects and all that. Stop pedalling and, unless you can do a damn good track stand, you'll come down. They are very useful for honing great balance (obviously) and upper body stillness whilst increasing cadence. DO NOT TRY GETTING OUT OF THE SADDLE AND SPRINTING UNLESS YOU ARE BLOODY GOOD ON THEM! You will end up out of the saddle, but not in the desired manner. As they are generally free flowing, they're not the best if you wish to do power work. For that you'll need a turbo trainer.

Turbos work by holding the bike in place and applying resistance. This can be done by running the back wheel on a resistant roller or by taking the wheel off and attaching the drivetrain directly to the unit. Many newer trainers are 'smart' so have software that can change resistance based on a computer program. You can pay under fifty pounds or over a thousand – there's a bewildering choice out there.

Turbos are great for power work, but you can also still do the high cadence, low power stuff that the rollers offer. However, because the bike is fixed to them, they cannot replicate that need to balance to stay upright. If you stop pedalling on a turbo trainer, you just get a rest.

So, rollers or turbo trainer: which is best? When, a few years ago, I broke my collarbone, I was obviously off the bike for about ten weeks. At the time, I owned just a set of rollers and, rollers being rollers, there was no way I was going to attempt to climb aboard with one arm in a sling. So, when I said that I was off the bike for about ten weeks, I was very much off the bike for that length of time.

Recently, I came off again and broke my wrist. I am sat here, typing this, arm in a cast, and looking out at an annoyingly sunny day – the kind of day that I would normally be out and about the lanes of Leafy Cheshire or even further afield. The difference is that now I own a turbo trainer and, because it locks the bike in place, the day after I got back from hospital, I was able to be back in the saddle. It's not the same as being out and about, obviously, but at least I can keep my fitness up. So, of the two, I think this shades it for the turbo.

(There are now turbo trainers that are able to simulate a climb – not only will they increase your resistance, but they will lift the front end in synchronicity. This means that we do not have to do stupid things like putting the rollers on the stairs to get the same effect, something that you rarely try more than once!)

It wasn't long before someone realised that turbo training, whilst a highly efficient way to get fit, was a bit, well, boring. Whatever the workout, anything over an hour spent looking at a wall in the garage could be a little mentally taxing, even if you were listening to music. Soon, videos were available on YouTube that you could watch whilst working out. You could follow someone up Alpe D'Huez or Ventoux, the Tourmalet or Aubisque, which made life a little more interesting. More structured content became available, which had specific training zones. Cyclists who did not have access to power meters or heart rate monitors could train to these zones using 'the rating of perceived exertion' (RPE), which is a system of self-analysis that runs from 1. super easy/comfortable to 10. maximum effort/take me off to hospital. I've also seen it running from 1 to 20, and other charts that run from 1 to 5 and from 1 to 7. The smart thing to do is to pick one, stick with that and, whatever you do, don't start swapping halfway through.

The advent of smart trainers and greater computer interactivity has allowed the whole system to become far more immersive, so much so, in fact, that it could take over from outdoor cycling in the minds of many. This raises an interesting point for me: I know a few people who regularly take part in gym spinning sessions but have never actually been on a real bike outside to ride - are they still cyclists? They're certainly pedalling, but their spinning machines are hardly 'bikes'. Riding a bike is so, so much more than this. Skip back a notch and could you then say that the moment I attach my road bike to a turbo trainer, I cease 'cycling' and begin simply 'training'? Certainly, this is how I view it and, as much as I appreciate that I am keeping fit, I would never consider this 'riding my bike'. The move away from the road, with all its inherent dangers, is also a move away from all the joys of the outside world and the pleasures that cycling brings. Take that away, and you're not really cycling anymore, are you?

Happily, you can partake in this hi-tech pain using relatively low-tech kit. I have a 'dumb trainer', costing about £200, which I've smartened up using a dongle and the interactivity of the sensors that came with the cycling computer. Once synced, even though I have to alter resistance (hence power) by changing gear on the bike, the computer app is able to use my speed and cadence to deduce power, showing it as 'virtual watts'. These virtual watts may not be spot on, they may not be my actual power output, but, as long as they are consistent with themselves, they are a more than adequate training tool. So, for example, if every reading it gives is 20 watts on the low side and it shows me that I have increased from 250 to 280 watts, I have still increased by thirty watts.

So, you've got your trainer, found a space for the pain cave, and you are ready to go: what can indoor riding offer you?

The answer is really, as with outdoor riding, as much or as little as you want it to. I find training indoors is great for a more structured session and, if you can't afford a power meter for the bike, using the trainer and apps to define your power can give you a measure of any improvements or (God forbid) losses in fitness. Heart rate monitors can help in this way too, but heart rate can sometimes be slightly misleading. As well a lag, where your heart will, in essence, be playing catch up with your efforts, your heart rate can be distorted by stress. I have watched mine go up during otherwise easy sessions when my mind has turned to something such as riding up Mow Cop or Winnats Pass. It went up once by 20bpm when I thought (thankfully wrongly) that the dogs were fighting downstairs. It shoots up if Shelly comes home while I'm training (make of that what you will), especially if I'm supposed to be outside cutting the hedge.

Although heart rate can be a less accurate barometer than power, it still has its place and is very useful when linked to power. Riding at the same power with a lower average heart rate, for instance, can be a good indicator of increased fitness.

I can end a session slipping from the saddle into an exhausted heap in the middle of the puddle of sweat I've produced, or I can ride easy for half an hour. Hard turbo sessions should be VERY HARD and easy ones, well, easy. All too often, we can fall in between, riding too easy on the hard spells and pushing too many watts on recovery rides. Remember, the easy rides are just as important. Hard turbo sessions (HIIT: high-intensity interval training) are also a great mental exercise. There are six mental stages you go through during a session. These are:

1. Ten minutes before: I'm going to do a session. Cool!
2. Warm up: This isn't so bad.
3. Ten minutes in: How am I going to keep this up for an hour?
4. Halfway through: OH MY GOD THIS IS HORRIBLE!
5. Final interval: I'M GONNA PUKE!
6. Ten minutes after finishing: That wasn't so bad. What's on the menu tomorrow?

The Theory of Cycling Relativity: Law 5
One minute of recovery is only half as long as one minute of interval.

Much like riding a long, steep hill, turbo sessions are a thing of the mind. Your body can take it, you just have to stop your mind getting in there and telling it otherwise. In order to get better, you have to suffer to some degree or another. Like that long hill, break the session down into mental chunks – it does get easier once you know that you're more than halfway through. It is also the nature of high intensity sessions that, once off the bike, your heart rate will drop back down, and you'll get your breath back within a relatively short time. There's nothing worse than bailing just before or during stage 5 only to realise afterwards that you could have completed it. It's like riding five miles up that hill only to put your foot down fifty yards from the summit.

My wife, hearing my suffering, will ask me why I put myself through it. "To make myself a better cyclist so that riding all those hills will be easier." "And are they?" "No. I just go up them quicker."* [*Greg LeMond was right: I've taken part in my favourite sportive, The Tour of the Peak, four times now, and finished each one equally physically wiped out and covered in roughly the same amount of snot, sticky gel and energy drink. Over the years, I have gradually taken over half an hour off my time for the 63-mile course.]

One of the hardest sessions you're likely to come across is the functional threshold power (FTP) test. The term FTP test can strike fear into the heart of all but the most masochistic cyclists. Essentially, it's the highest average power you can put out over the course of an hour. Mercifully, an FTP test can be done over twenty minutes, the result being taken as 95% of your output over that time. It is still bloody hard though.

Why do it? It sets a benchmark or baseline from which all your following sessions can be worked out. Then, later, after you have spent weeks or months working very hard, you can do it again to see by how much you've (hopefully) progressed. It is not something one looks forward to.

I explained this process to Shelly, who asked:

"Well, if you've got better, shouldn't it be easier the second time around?"

"Er, no, that's not the point. It will be just as hard."

She then came in for a chat halfway through the FTP, just to see how I was getting on, and quickly left, miffed that I wasn't really engaging with her.

You don't need a computer program to do workouts. If you're into watching your football, cricket or rugby, you can set up the trainer for a televised match and do your high intensity intervals every time the ball goes out of play. To increase the frequency, simply add every rugby scrum, every boundary in cricket or every time a player falls over in football.

It's not just about the tough stuff. I use my indoor trainer for gentle recovery rides because this is not something that I have been able to master outside. Riding on the road can be more difficult than you'd like it to be, even at the best of times and, unless you live by an endless, gentle downslope that will bring you right back to your door, road riding can be downright incompatible with recovery. You have headwinds, you have gradients, you have that guy up the road that you just have to catch. All these things are vying to turn a recovery ride into just another ride. On the trainer, there are none of these distractions, and I can happily sit at a steady cadence, pushing as little as 100 watts for an hour (whilst listening to something nice and mellow like Nick Drake or Dire Straits). No sweat: literally.

If you want to do specific cycle training, the best course of action is to use a structured training plan, or a coach (in person or online) who can provide you with something tailored to your own needs.

7. OUTDOOR TRAINING

I am happy training to power and heart rate inside, but I am not remotely interested in riding to power on the road and seldom wear my HR monitor outside of my pain cave. Why not? We see countless pictures of pros riding along whilst staring at their computers so it must be important, right? For them, it's obviously important for rider and team to see their data. I suppose it's also a mental aid to show them that, yes, they can ride up this bit of road at 400 watts for the next thirty-seven and a half minutes. For the rest of us, especially if we are not racing, even if we could hold that power for that time, we might then be truly knackered for the rest of the ride. Just because the numbers tell you what you can do, it doesn't necessarily mean that that's what you should do.

My outlook is to train inside so that I can cycle out. I rarely, if ever, take the bike out on the road with the view to doing a bit of training – that would just spoil the ride! However, there's many a ride that starts out easy and ends with me battering myself into the ground. (This is especially true with a sportive, which isn't meant to be a race, but always turns out that way.) On the road, I ride on feel: I am well aware if I'm busting a gut to get up a hill or soft pedalling along a flat and I don't need a computer to tell me that. For me, the outdoors is just too subject to variables to be made sense of by metrics. Those things that can ruin my recovery ride will also impact on the hard stuff. It's not just recovery or high intensity. Mixed terrain, weather conditions and company can have an effect on any targeted training you might want to do. Building an endurance base, for example, is best done at a low intensity, but intended 'structured' endurance rides can be fraught with the need to blast up short hills or keep up with a faster mate when a much easier pace is called for. Importantly for me, for the vast majority of my outdoor cycling, training is the very last thing on my mind, and even these endurance building rides can be done on my trainer.

Very occasionally, though, I will train outside, and pick a local hill to ride up and down repeatedly like an idiot, going flat out. I don't need a power meter to tell me what 'flat out' is. All I need to know is that I am giving it everything, and 'flat out' will change from day to day, depending upon how I'm feeling, or whether I'm riding into a headwind, or whatever. It might be 600 watts one day and 450 another, but it will always be flat out. Doing just this on a nearby short (500m) ramp a few years ago I was stopped about half an hour in by an assistant from the children's adventure farm at the bottom of the hill.
"The children want to know what you're doing."
"It's called hill repeats. It's to make me get better at riding up hills."
"Oh," she said, "I guess it's not working, then. They've been timing you: they said to tell you that you're getting slower."

Obviously, if you are planning to race, training outside is very much a necessity: you can't mimic road tactics or fast cornering on an indoor trainer (not without unfortunate results). Even if you just want to get that little bit fitter, structured sessions – indoors or out – work a treat, but be careful, because it's all too easy to get bogged down in the numbers and forget why you started riding in the first place.

It's also true that we can get so caught up in training that we can overtrain (it's a thing!) and push ourselves so much that it leads to a plateau or even fall off in performance. There is no doubt that HIIT works, but it can have negative effects if you're not careful. I've had some great results during tough midweek training sessions, hitting all my power numbers, only to roll up for my Sunday group ride feeling like I've finished it before I've even started. It's actually very easy to overtrain when you're so intent on working hard to improve, and more, more, more is not necessarily better. It's important to remember:

The Theory of Cycling Relativity: Law 6
Sometimes, it's better not to ride.

Rather than hitting every session as hard as you can, mix it up a bit. I probably do no more than two HIIT sessions per week now, preferring to ride easy the rest of the time, and I usually have one day off the bike altogether. This works for me, and keeps me at a level I'm happy with.

8. RIDING UP HILLS

As I said earlier, hard training sessions are about pain – pushing the limits both physically and mentally. And, if you can conquer a psychological mountain, it is much easier to conquer that physical one.

Riding up hills is great, but there's one inherent problem with hills: every bloody one seems to be beset by some sort of slope or - the term more commonly used these days - gradient. Unless you live somewhere ridiculously flat, like Cambridgeshire, and never envision riding far from your home, these gradients are a constant part of a cyclist's life and, just like life in general, with every up there's a down, and wherever there's a down there will, inevitably, be an up waiting around the corner.

On the world stage, we can watch the professionals race up huge mountain passes. It never looks easy, even though the television does tend to flatten out the image. (Sometimes, the only way to gauge the steepness of an incline is to compare it to the people or houses on it that, for the most part, should be standing vertically.) It is perhaps bizarre that, watching these superhuman athletes as they fight their battle with gravity, your thoughts should turn to "I want to do that!", and it is one of the joys of our sport that we can go off and ride those very same roads ourselves.

However, unless you are lucky/unlucky (delete as applicable) to actually live on or close to a famous incline, everybody's experience of hills begins with the local climb. This may not be particularly long, or steep, but it nevertheless provides us with a challenge. As a youngster, mine was riding from the bottom of my road up, past the old, disused chapel (now apartments), and then left, up the steep bit, to the top. It, as is the way these days, is a segment now and is, apparently, 0.42km at an average of 7% (at points 12 and 13%). This would have meant little to me as a kid in the 1970s: for a start, everything was in miles, and hills were always one in something or other. I just knew it was tough and it was an achievement to get to the top without stopping. Dad certainly never took the caravan that way to the motorway when we went away on holidays.

I am quite lucky where I live, here in Leafy Cheshire. There's lots of easily accessible countryside that's generally gently rolling but even here there are plenty of ups and downs to be had as, now and again, the sandstone bed, upon which the boulder clay of the plain lies, forms outcrops. This gives us areas, dotted about here and there, with short, stiff hills. Where we live, near Leafy Lymm, is on top of one such outcrop. The Cheshire Plain starts just to the south of our house and laps up against the Welsh border thirty miles to the west and the southern Pennines and the Peak District about twenty to the east. Usually my rides on this relatively level ground are mere commutes (mostly eastwards) to get me over to a lumpier playground.

These are what I think of as my local climbs. They are nowhere near the alpine passes that some would class as 'proper' climbs but they're no less tough because of it. Most are around about a kilometre, but it is the average gradient that hurts – 7 to 10%. We have a couple of longer pulls with slightly shallower slopes, namely Snake Pass and Cat & Fiddle, but these are the exceptions to the rule that is short, sharp and shock. Most of the ups are struggles and the downs, sadly, are usually too short and/or twisty to make up for it. This is simply the lay of the land.

There are two climbs in my area that still fill me with dread – Winnats Pass and, further south, Mow Cop. Both are absolute brutes, not due to their length, but their gradients, with sustained pitches of 20% on both. It is also the mental torture approaching them that really has an effect. The Winnats road disappears up in between two limestone walls, this natural theatre adding to its sense of foreboding. Mow Cop, though, is more obvious in its intent. If you haven't been there, imagine a child's drawing of a castle on a hill, with a road right up the middle of it – that's Mow Cop. Approaching it from the north, you can see this line of tarmac going seemingly vertically up the hill and, immediately, your legs get tired and you start to feel the hamstring injury from fifteen years ago you had, until now, long forgotten about. I've ridden up both a few times, I know I can do it, so they should hold no fear – but they do.

The Theory of Cycling Relativity: Law 7
It's all in the mind.

Hills, like seemingly endless turbo sessions, are all in the mind. There are very few of them knocking about that you can't physically crest, unless you've made some sort of spectacular blunder by coming out to play on a single speed bike. Even those that are most daunting at first can be broken up into mental chunks and ticked off. Actually, longer climbs can be mentally easier to tackle because you're usually psychologically prepared for the worst before you've even begun. The mighty Ventoux is one example, where the climb is marked by stones every kilometre, counting down to the top. Halfway through, deep into its forêt interminable, I got a massive mental kick when I realised that it actually was not half the demon I had imagined it would be, and I knew that I could grind my way up. (I was also spurred on no end by the cloud of flies I had accumulated on the way up. If I were to stop, it would give them somewhere to land, so there was no way I was going to hang around. At one point, I thought I might ride alongside another cyclist – to chat etc – but her flying fan club was far bigger than mine, so I kept my distance.)

The thing is, hills hurt, so why do we want to ride them? It is probably that feeling of achievement that stays with us. I love riding up hills because it's hard, not in spite of the fact. It gives a ride more of a meaning and, even if I'm on a supposedly easy local spin around Leafy Cheshire, I will invariably end up at the base of a hill or two and then, well, it would be churlish not to, wouldn't it? Hills are 'event moments' that punctuate the ride. Riding around on flat road might be, well, nice, but it doesn't really give you much to talk about when you get back other than the fact that you had a nice ride. Throw in a steep hill or two and you've been an absolute hero!

It seems that many of us are drawn to hills, like a moth to the flame and, even if we don't relish a climb, a ride would not be a ride without one or two thrown in. A friend who I ride with often draws up our route a couple of days beforehand. Rule of thumb is that we ride up and down lots of hills to a coffee stop, before riding up and down more hills to get home.
Cruising alongside him one morning, early on in the ride, I could hear him muttering, "I f*****g hate hills."
"Hang on a mo, Ken," I said, "you decide the route. If you don't like hills, why do you keep bringing us up them?"
"Aye," he said, "and I don't like ham sandwiches either, but I made them for breakfast."

I'll quite happily cycle twenty-five miles with the sole intention of riding up a certain short, steep hill, and then cycle the twenty-five miles back home again. I suppose it gives a ride a focus: that focus being, "Yay! I'm going to ride a long way so I can hurt myself for a few minutes!"

Hills are funny things. Put one half a mile from your door and you'll likely skip up it like the mountain goat you always imagined you were. Put that same hill forty hard miles away and it can become almost insurmountable. It's not the hill's fault, of course, it's because our odd little bodies are subject to fatigue. Ride at even a moderately easy pace, holding a constant power, and you'll notice that your heart rate will inevitably begin to creep up (unless you're super fit...or dead): you're doing the same work, but fatigue is affecting you. Put yourself on a long hill with a constant gradient – an Alp, if you're lucky! – and you'll find that you're much more tired the further up the climb you go, even though you're effectively putting in the same power. You have to work harder to stay the same.
For this reason:

The Theory of Cycling Relativity:
Law 8
The longer the ride, the harder the hill is at the end of it.

So, plan accordingly.

As we are all of differing abilities, ride the hills to your own strengths and not to anyone else's. It will do you no good to try and hold the wheel of a much better rider at the bottom of a climb only to drop off and die (ideally, metaphorically) halfway up. This is especially true in sportives, where you might find yourself riding with a group of strangers.

In our weekend group, everyone rides the gradients at their own pace and then we regroup at the top. Being of racing snake physique, I am one of the faster climbers, but I am no match for Lee. Most climbs we will begin riding together but then, almost imperceptibly, he will drift off and away. We could be in the middle of a conversation and, suddenly, he is ahead without seeming to do more work. And then he saunters away and is gone until the top. I know from experience that there is no point hanging on – although trying has made me a better rider – and so I spend the rest of the climb trying to keep his backside within view.

"Hey, Lee, when do you know you've dropped me?"

"I can't hear you breathing anymore."

At the same time, because I'm riding to my own pace, I can't sit up and wait for the guys behind. It's much easier, although lonelier, tapping out my own cadence, dangling betwixt and between.

One ride, there was just the two of us on a lumpy route through the Peak District around Macclesfield. It consisted of us reaching a hill, where Lee would do his drifting away thing and I'd struggle (but still be graceful as an ibex, obviously) up it after him. At the top, I'd find him waiting and suitably rested and, as I got there, he'd set off and ride away towards the next climb, dragging me with him, where the whole process would be repeated. This meant that the guy who didn't really need the break was getting lots and the one who was desperate for it wasn't getting any. He'd make a great coach.

Why, then? Why do some of us love hurting ourselves on steep roads? Here's the take of Simon Warren, a rider of hills and author of the "100 Climbs" series of books.

"Much like most things in life my journey to cycling was an amalgamation of chance encounters and circumstances, each a piece of a puzzle that when complete formed the perfect whole. I wasn't born to ride a bike, I didn't come from a cycling family, nor did I have athletic genes but, through a series of key events, I discovered the greatest pastime on the planet.

Like most kids growing up in the '70s and '80s I was never without two wheels, everyone in our village had a bike and, no matter what brand, or what condition, we treasured them. Each machine was an extension of its rider, a collection of mechanical siblings that accompanied us on our adventures. Some had brand new BMXs, some Grifters, Choppers, some hand-me-downs, and then the bigger kids in the village rode Bombers or occasionally proper racers. When I say proper, I mean lightweight, impossibly thin tyres, 12 gears, toeclips etc, and the mere sight of these exotic machines would make my heart flutter. They were the supercars of our scene, unobtainable and intoxicating.

Roll on ten years, though. After a childhood of saving pennies I decided I would spend some of my horde and, following much deliberation, some haggling and parental assistance, I purchased the item I had coveted all those years ago, a racing bike. My new Raleigh Corsa had indexed gears, SLR brakes, Biopace chainrings, Reynolds 531 tubing and, most importantly of all, super skinny 21mm tyres. That impossibly narrow rubber that had so excited me years earlier was now, almost unbelievably in my possession. I had no inclination to race it though – that thought never even entered my mind – I simply wanted the bike, to own and to polish it. Maybe I'd flash it up and down the village sometimes to make sure everyone could see how far I'd come, but then I'd put it right back in my bedroom before it got dirty.

By chance, around the same time, another lad in the village had also procured a racing bike and we did eventually end up going on a few rides, because really, there is no point in owning a Ferrari if you're never going to drive it, right? And that's what it felt like. After 17 years of old heavy clunkers, this svelte, lightweight machine went like sh*t off a shovel. Hurtling down the lane out the back of our village, the sunlight bounced off its lustrous finish and polished components, the tyres, pumped hard, pinged off the tarmac, and with my feet in the toeclips I could power it to speeds I never previously thought possible.

Around this time at school, towards the end of my GCSEs and the beginning of A-levels, it was a time of change. My friends were all growing up fast, and old-fashioned fun had been replaced by cheap booze, smoking, drugs, going to see bands, nightclubs and rebellion. The thing is, for a myriad of reasons I wanted nothing to do with this and now my bike was going to be MY source of rebellion from the herd mentality of my peers. I've never been a loner – I love company, an audience to play to – but I have always been individual. I never wanted to do what the crowd did, listen to the popular music the crowd listened to. (I would turn up at teenage parties with my personal stereo and headphones on so I could listen to Zeppelin and AC/DC whist all the sheep danced to the Cure and the Smiths.)

So, I was going to go my own way, I was going to ride my bike, I was going to improve my body, not destroy it (I left that for my 20s). Still, it was all without direction or purpose until my Uncle David turned up. I knew he was a cyclist, and we had been laughing at the outfits he wore for a few years now. "Do the pixies know you have been raiding their wardrobe, David?" was a typical taunt when he would come and say hello to my mum. He lived just up the road and his garage was an Aladdin's Cave of exotica. He was also bloody fast, the local club's best time trialist, so, the one day he turned up and said, "Son, you're coming racing tomorrow night" and preceded to tell me where and when, there would be NO debate.

I'd never been touring, never joined a cycling club and here I was about to head off onto a busy dual carriageway to mix it up with the giant wagons hurtling between Long Bennington to

Grantham, and in a ten-mile time trial too. I had my number pinned on, I took my slot in the line waiting to start and my Uncle came along to deliver his pep talk. He took my water bottle out of its cage and threw it in the grass verge. He took the spare tube and banana out of my pockets and tossed them aside. "Lad, it's ten miles, you don't need any of this crap. You grab the drops, you don't let go and you pedal as hard as you can to the roundabout and come back." That was it. With my instructions I waited for the countdown: 3, 2, 1, and I went. I'd never ridden in anger before, I really had no idea what I was doing, and I returned a time of 28.53. Upon looking at my time, the club's elders knew instantly I was not a talent - it really is as simple as that - but gave encouragement all the same. Next week I was back, now knowing the drill, and did 25.54. I went back the next week, and the next, in fact I never missed an 'evening ten' for four years.

I loved the competition, at first to just beat myself, and then to try and beat everyone else, and I loved the people. I'd tried my hand at a few sports, in fact I'd been pretty handy with a badminton racket and a hockey stick but, as soon as I set eyes on the mismatch of riders lined up in this small village just off the A1, I knew they looked like the crowd I wanted to belong to. Everyone fits in somewhere and I was to find that the cycling club was the perfect place for me. There was not a bad egg amongst them. No attitude, no violence, no arrogance, and so another couple of pieces of the jigsaw had fallen into place.

Roll on to the end of that summer and I get my first taste of a hill climb on Terrace Hill. I'd got to grips with the 10-mile time trial, but this was going to be something else altogether. I knew the hill – everyone knew the hill – but I wasn't lining up with any delusions of victory, it was just another time trial, and I couldn't get enough of time trials! I was still in the junior category and there was a clear favourite for the event: he had already taken the junior 10 and 25 titles and just needed this for the hat-trick.

He hadn't bargained for me though – no one had. Somehow, I flew up that hill and got my hands on my first ever trophy, and now I had really found my calling. It mattered not that I only beat a tiny handful of riders - suddenly I was a winner. I graduated the following year to take the first of my senior club titles but alas this would be the pinnacle of my achievements. When I had to race riders from other clubs in open events, I never got higher than the second step. All the same, I loved the hills, I loved racing the hill climbs: the atmosphere, the stripped-down bike. I could manage a top ten in most local events and that was more than enough motivation to rip myself apart each weekend.

The final part which would bind my life to cycling came from the tv and Channel 4's coverage of the Tour de France. During that first summer of time trialling on the A1, the American Greg Lemond was battling the Frenchman Laurent Fignon in the greatest race of all time. A real-life sporting soap opera was playing out each evening and it culminated in the most fantastic outpouring of emotion I'd witnessed in my life. The joy, the pure joy of Lemond winning on that final stage struck me so hard in the heart it started a fire burning that will never go out. I had fallen in love with the bicycle, I had fallen in love with racing a bicycle and now I had fallen in love with watching others do it, this was what I wanted to do forever."

For competitive types, hills are, like other riders, or like the clock, there to be beaten. They are an immovable foe. They can be complete bastards, but they do have a good side...

9. RIDING DOWN HILLS!

Hills illustrate to me the great difference between cycling as a child and cycling now. Now, the great accomplishment is riding up them, back then, it was going the other way. As a child, after managing to master staying upright on two wheels, this hurtling downhill at top speed was the great thrill of riding a bike. Everywhere we went, riding was not about, as it is now, conquering the ups, but about flying down the downs. We'd happily push our bikes to the top of a road to then risk life and limb to descend as fast as we could.

The estate where we lived, Oldfield Brow, was built on the side of a hill, so we had plenty of choice. Our road was a slope, at the top of which was the fearsome Cobbles. Dropping down from the top of The Cobbles without touching the brakes was a skill that had to be learnt. Another road, down the middle of the estate, was a series of three ramps, levelling out twice before the bottom where other roads crossed it. It was (and still is) called Greenway. To us, it was "The Three Hills", a place to build up speed and test your nerve. Alternatively, you could race down the longer Oldfield Road from the top of the estate to The Conker Trees at the bottom. Everything was about going down as fast as you could.

The local park, half a mile away, was on the other side of the same geological lump and so was similarly strewn with slopes that, when we weren't playing footy, we were riding down.

Downhill riding was the thing! That was the test, and going up was not at all important, other than it was just a way of getting to the start. So, now fast forward, and the downhill bit, although the prize, is not the raison d'être.

We watch the pros flying off Alps at top speed during Le Tour and it looks fantastic but these guys are very good bike handlers, ride on generally well-surfaced roads, do not have to worry too much about the vehicles coming the other way, and so can use the whole width of tarmac to pick their lines. It's a bit different from dropping down into Buxton on the rutted A537 on a wet winter's morning when all the gravel wagons are out in force.

As much as going up requires physical and mental fortitude, so does descending. Riding a downhill, especially a long one, is tough on the arms and on the concentration. (If I could have a downhill head song it would probably be Ultravox's "Young Savage" but I'm usually far too busy looking down the road for the next bend/car/pothole/ errant sheep, etc.) The

Theory of Cycling Relativity:
Law 9
Shouting "Weeeeeeee!!!" when descending does not make you go any faster, but it is more fun.

Many who have not ridden for a long time or who have recently taken up cycling might find going down just as hard, if not harder, as going up.

The speed you can very quickly reach on a modern road bike can be a shock to the system, particularly when you can see the need to brake hard fast approaching. It can be scary.

As much as it's an important fact that the way to get good at riding up is to ride up a lot, the same holds true for descending but, unlike uphill, downhill cannot be practiced on a turbo trainer (even if you put one on a slope). The ability to descend has to be learnt out on the road: how to ride at speed, how to lose that speed when necessary, cornering etc. You need to hone these skills and then trust them - it's amazing how many times I have seen riders come off on hills simply by trying to be too careful. Over-braking can cause the bike to lock up or skid (as I have found to my cost), so learn how to pick your line and trust that the bike will do its job. Lack of braking is also dangerous because it can cause you to go straight on where you don't really want to. It's also a fact that many crashes are caused by people focusing so much on the object they're trying to avoid that they drive (yes, motorists have accidents too) or ride into it, so always look to where you want to go, not where you don't.

Descending is all about confidence, so build it up on easier slopes, those with gentle drops or few corners, those that you know like the back of your hand. Learn what your bike can do. When you've nailed the simpler stuff, try a steeper, or longer, or twistier venue. But ride within your abilities. Essentially, it's the same idea as sticking to the nursery slopes while you try to stay upright on your skis and staying well off the black run.

The last thing you want is to find yourself in a situation where you scare yourself silly riding down a hill or, worse still, come off, because:

The Theory of Cycling Relativity: Law 10
Falling off does not do wonders for your confidence.

Always stay well within your limits and don't push it until you are confident enough. Practice, practice, practice.

Also, do not forget to pedal. It might seem an odd reminder, but it's all too easy to freewheel a descent. In doing this, legs that have been working very hard to get up to the top will quickly begin to stiffen up (this is why it's best to do a warm down spin following a tough ride/training session). Given that many downhills are followed by uphills, the last thing you want when the road starts turning skyward again is heavy limbs. Keep turning those cranks. Even if you find yourself going so fast that you're spinning out, keep turning those cranks.

Downhills, like everything else, are not immune to being ruined by a headwind. It is one of life's travesties when the great payoff of free speed and the feeling of flying you have earned by slogging up one side of a long hill does not come to pass, and you stop pedalling only to find that your bike grinds to a halt. It's hugely galling, having expended all that energy getting to the top, to find that you have to continue doing so to get down the other side. I once crested a hill to be met with such a wall of wind that I was forced to pedal down a 10% slope in my smallest gear. It was not fun. Fortunately, it only lasted a mile before I could turn off to find the comparative respite of another climb.

THE WOBBLES
As if we don't get enough near-death experiences, what with cars, potholes or squirrels, cycling throws us a physics curve ball with the phenomenon that is the speed wobble. This is a frightening something that can happen when you are usually enjoying a downhill. Suddenly, the front end of your bike starts to judder as if someone else has got hold of the bars and is giving them a shake. The vibration goes right through the length of the bike and it feels as if you are going to be thrown off by this unseen force. That you are going at faster speeds at a time when you feel like you are losing control of your bike does not do anything for your confidence.

There are a few different theories as to why this happens, from loose headsets to poorly manufactured frames to incorrect rider position. Oddly, when it's happened to me (twice), it has been on smooth and relatively straight descents, so I don't think prevailing road conditions come into it. Also, you are not likely to get a 'wobble black spot', where the bike tries to get away from you every time you ride down the same bit of road.

Whatever the reasons, these are not thoughts that go through your head at the time and the instinct is to stiffen up, hold on tight, and even try to immediately slow or stop the bike with the brakes. Actually, the best thing to do is to try and relax, not grip the bar too tightly, push your weight forward (which increases load on the front end), and let the bike ride itself out of the issue. Gently pressing your knees against the top tube also seems to have a positive effect. I have read that you can help by putting your feet at a twelve-six o'clock position. This loads the 'six' pedal and lowers the centre of gravity, increasing stability. I have also read that you should lift your bum off your seat, which is not a wholly natural thing to do while your feet are at twelve-six. This is also a lot to think about in what can be a moment of panic. If you want to make an attempt at slowing down, gently feathering the rear brake until you have mastered the wobble appears to be the favoured technique.

In both my instances, although shaken (both physically and mentally), I managed to correct the issue without braking. Since then, I ride down any steep inclines using the 'knees against the top tube' method and have been incident free and, touch carbon, will remain so.

The slight problem in the UK is the short nature of many of our steeper hills. The point when you ideally need to let the bike run freely is often the point that you can see the bottom of the hill fast approaching and the sharp bend, junction or, as has happened to me at such a time, group of ramblers and their dogs strewn across the road, that lie there. Thus, there is a very definite need to apply the brakes sometime soon or risk going straight on into somewhere or someone you shouldn't.

Cycling's nothing if not exciting!

10. CADENCE AND GEARS

When I was a kid, there was a man who used to cycle past our house twice a day. I would ride alongside him on my little blue Raleigh as best as I could but I could never figure out how he could be pedalling more slowly than me but moving faster. Every time I tried to match his cadence (I didn't know what that was back then) he would quickly drift away. I was baffled. The reason, of course, was gears!

Many have a misconception that the reason there are gears on your bike is to make you go faster. Obviously, pushing a larger gear along a level or downhill road at the same cadence, this might be true, but the actual reason there are gears on a bike is to make your life easier. It's an important distinction because the two mindsets could be the difference between you grinding to a halt on a climb (or into a stiff headwind) and continuing to inch forward. Don't let pride get in the way of efficiency by trying to 'big ring' it up a climb, only to find yourself running out of steam halfway up. All your gears are there to be used, so use them. Yes, even the 'granny gear'!

Much has been written about 'the perfect cadence' and it appears that this ideal stroke is 90rpm. The thing is, we are all different and, while 90rpm might be fine and dandy for one person – or even the vast majority – it might not work well for you.

The best way to discover your ideal cadence is to spin away on your trainer whilst wearing a heart rate monitor and nail the point at which, after a good warm up, you feel comfortable turning the pedals at a certain speed or power wattage. Stick at the same speed/power but try turning up the revs, and watch your heart rate. If it rises, it's an indicator that you're having to work harder and so the cadence is less efficient. If it stays the same, or even drops slightly, it shows that you are more efficient pedalling at that speed. The same will be true if you up the gears and try churning away at a lower cadence. Each change in cadence will have an effect on your body's capacity to keep to it.

Because we are all different, this ideal number will be different. Some have thighs like tree trunks and ample power to turn the cranks in a bigger gear, but might start to suffer when called upon to pedal faster. Others, with lighter builds, may find it easier to spin away. These different physiology and muscle types will require their own 'ideal' strokes.

Watching the professionals ride, especially up hills, there has been a sea change from the past fashion of grinding massive gears to the hummingbird spinning style of Chris Froome and his chums more recently. Ah, you might think, so that's the way to go! But you must remember that these guys are highly trained athletes with cardiovascular systems that can cope with the demands of sustained high cadences and most of us are a long way from being highly trained athletes, no matter how fit we think we are. And actually, if you watch a group of pro riders, particularly on a mountain stage, nobody is pedalling at the same rate because they all have their own cadences at which they're most comfortable and efficient. If there was a perfect cadence, they'd all be on it.

The Theory of Cycling Relativity: Law 11
The bigger gear is not always the faster gear.

Gears are there to make our lives better and it's pointless pushing a big one when a smaller, easier one will do. Much like the engine in a car, there is always the right gear for the occasion. You might think that the easier the gear, the easier the ride, but that does not automatically follow. Choose the wrong gear in your car – too low and it will over rev, too high and it will stall – and the engine is inefficient. And so it goes with you and your bike.

This is especially true when changing gears. Whatever your cadence is, try and keep it constant. If you start to pedal too quickly, it means that you should change up (again, just like changing gear in a car when revs rise) and, should you feel like you're pedalling through custard, change down into an easier gear. It helps greatly if you can anticipate your coming speed and smoothly alter gear accordingly. This way, you'll not get to the bottom of a steep hill and find yourself massively overgeared, requiring a number of rapid changes that your bike will likely noisily protest. As well as sounding appalling, the sudden change of rhythm can bring you almost to a halt. Never enjoy that downhill into a valley so much that you leave yourself totally unprepared to get up the other side.

I saw this happen to devastating effect on a local sportive as a rider dived past me down into a steep valley. The road crossed a bridge and then immediately hairpinned up at over 20%. The chap hit this sudden change of direction and incline, slammed his brakes on, and then tried to pedal out of the dip but, having scrubbed off all his speed and leaving himself in far too high a gear, he simply ground to an immediate halt and keeled over. I carefully (and ever-so-slightly smugly) rode around him.

I think he was okay.

The Theory of Cycling Relativity: Law 12
Find the cadence that is right for you.

The big thing is to find the cadence that is right for you and not concentrate too much on making you fit a cadence. Like much in cycling, it's all too easy to get caught up in the science. Chances are, it won't be too far away from that magic 90 anyway since, even if you have the chunkiest thighs in the world, constantly grinding a huge gear will start to fatigue you before too long and you'll be forced into changing down to a more forgiving gear. And, the more you ride, the fitter you'll become, and it should be a natural progression that you'll find yourself pedalling a little faster and more fluidly.

I GOT RHYTHM*
If you're riding a hill, particularly if you're doing it alone, it can be a great thing to have a head song, something that you can mentally sing along to that helps you tap out a cadence. Obviously, different songs have different beats, and it's important to find one or two that fit your cadence rather than the other way around.
There's no point picking a tune that has 110bpm when your climbing cadence is a steady 85rpm. My own personal earworms are Love's "Alone Again Or..." and "Something For The Weekend" by The Divine Comedy so, if you're knocking about The Peak District and hear the faint strains of "She said...there's something in the woodshed...", it's probably I, The Flying Goat of Leafy Cheshire, scourging yet another incline.

What you don't want is a song with a variable rhythm. The Beatles' "A Day In The Life" or Queen's "Bohemian Rhapsody", great songs and classics both, would not be ideal for tapping out a cadence, unless, by some amazing geographical fluke, you found roads with gradients that would fit their beat.

MY TOP 5 BANGING HILL-THEMED HEAD TUNES & THEIR APPROXIMATE CADENCES!
1. "Break On Through To The Other Side", by The Doors (90rpm).
2. "Reward", The Teardrop Explodes (80rpm).
3. "Shout To The Top", The Style Council (70rpm).
4. "Up Around The Bend", Creedence Clearwater Revival (70rpm).
5. "Waterfall", The Stone Roses (53rpm going up, or 105rpm coming down).
[*My music taste might be very 'last century', but they're classics, right??!!]

11. WEATHER

It is a fact that there is actually no 'bad' weather – there is just weather. It's always there. Oh, you have blazing sun, torrential rain, gale force winds, hail the size of golf balls, black ice, snizzle (it's a thing), plagues of locusts, the lot, but it's all just weather. Whether or not it's bad weather depends upon how ready you are for it. Most weather decisions can be made thus:

1. It looks rainy/snowy/windy tomorrow, so I'll have a lie in and maybe go on the trainer.

This can create a problem because, the one thing we know about weather is that it can be fickle and capricious, and there's a very good chance that whatever the nice weatherperson said after the news, when the morning comes, it will be bright and sunny. Other cyclists will be out and about while you have missed your chance and are on the way to the supermarket or garden centre. You may well have had an extra hour or two in bed but will spend the day regretting it. MAKE YOUR DECISION AS LATE AS POSSIBLE!

2. You get up early for your ride and the weather actually is rainy/snowy/windy.

Now you have a decision to make. If you're riding with friends, put it out to the group - it's much easier to let one of them decide and you can praise/berate them later depending upon which way it went. If you choose to ride, two things could happen: it gets better or it gets worse.

3. The weather gets better.
This is great! although it means that you may end up having to take off and carry all the gear you've put on to keep the weather out. This is why cycling kit is made to fold up into your back pocket. And you have three pockets.

4. The weather gets worse.
One thing about cycling psychology is that, once you're out, it doesn't matter what the weather's doing, you're more than likely to stay out. And, if the weather really takes a turn for the worse it can actually be a positive thing because this will turn what might have been a mere spin in the drizzle with your mates into AN EPIC!!!!

Epics can come in many shapes and sizes, but they are mostly defined by the weather. Think of the EPIC RIDES in recent pro cycling history. There have been many that were incredibly long, or mountainous, but the ones that stick in the memory are the cold and the wet: think Hinault's Liege win in 1980, or Hampsten taking the Maglia Rosa on the Gavia in 1988, or me making the bad decision to leave the waterproofs in the car for that sportive in October 2017.
Every year, most cycling fans pray for an epically wet Paris-Roubaix - as if that race wasn't tough enough! We can all have epic rides, too. Those ones you can look back on and recall happily such moments as, "Remember when that snow

plough turned back but we keep going!" or laughingly reminisce about "the time that we stopped off for coffee: I was so cold and wet that I was shivering so much I couldn't hold the cup!" At the time, epic rides tend to be the most horrible, miserable affairs but misery often makes a memory that the very same ride in pleasant sunshine does not. It's the cyclist's version of the campfire tale.

The Theory of Cycling Relativity: Law 13
Some rides can be so bad that they become EPIC, which is great!

HEADWIND
Firstly, headwind is not trying so hard you fart through your ears. I have done this, and that is another thing entirely. Headwind is the scourge of the cyclist. Rain, you can wear a coat. Cold, you can put on extra layers. But wind... well, even the warmest, sunniest day can be ruined.
Common sense will tell you that, on any circular route, there will be a time when the wind is sometimes from the front, sometimes from the side, and sometimes from behind. Sadly, this does not seem to be the case. It might happen occasionally – I hear tell of a mythical tailwind that occasionally gets up on the A50 just outside Knutsford (after a full moon) – but, for most of the time, we cyclists have to contend with a headwind. It accompanies us just as that cloud of dust follows Charlie Brown's pal Pig-Pen and is just about as welcome. Any day that you look

out of the window and see a mere flutter of leaves on the trees, you know you're going to be in for a hard time.

If Mother Nature was not enough, we also have physics to contend with, because every time you ride your bike, you're up against air drag or wind resistance. It's like your own personal headwind. Even if there is no breeze, as soon as you start, you create one by virtue of your own forward motion (unless you ride everywhere backwards). The faster you ride, the higher the resistance is, and the more personal headwind you're creating. That's why, on a still day, there's still a mad wind rushing past your ears when you're bombing downhill. It follows that, the better you get at riding, the faster you go (which seems great), but the faster you go, the tougher it is, because the headwind that you are creating is ever greater. This is what gives us one of our more obvious points:

The Theory of Cycling Relativity:
Law 14
Riding fast is much harder than riding slow.

This is the reason why we can all ride a bike for an hour, but most of us can't ride anywhere near the fifty-five or so kilometres per hour that Victor Campenaerts rode to break the hour record in April 2019. [Me: I'm going to watch the hour record on the telly. Shelly: Okay. How long's it on for?] He was in nigh on ideal conditions, indoors and so with no natural headwind to put up with and, although he was wearing the slipperiest kit and riding the most aerodynamic bike, the amount of sustained power needed to push through that wind resistance was massive.

So, headwind is our enemy, but it is one that we have to grudgingly put up with – unless we can find a large pal who's happy to let us ride behind him all day – especially if we want to ride faster. And, if we want to ride faster, we need to get aero. The problem is that getting aero is all well and good – you could pay some money and go and sit in a wind tunnel (on your bike, obviously, or it'd be a fun waste of time), or just work your 'aeroness' out in the mirror – but it does not necessarily follow that you will ride faster. This is because cycling is full of trade-offs, and one of them is that putting yourself in a fantastic, scrunched up position to cheat the wind might possibly prevent you from turning the cranks as efficiently as you were when you were sitting more comfortably upright. Let's face it, if super aero was the way to be, we'd all be pootling about on time trial bikes. So, much like losing a bit of weight, you have to be careful not to change to your own detriment and, rather than attempting to get your chin down to your front tyre, look to find a Goldilocks* position.
[* Just right!]

RAIN

The problem with rain.

Rain is wet.

This is a problem if you're looking out of the window at a downpour and thinking that it's probably a rest day. It's a problem if you are already out, it's cold and it begins to rain and your rain jacket is still in the drawer at home (see "Cold", a little further on). It's a problem because it produces puddles that (a) hide potholes, (b) make cornering less fun, and (c) find their way into your face from the rider in front or any passing vehicle. And, it's a problem because, after all that, you'll have a bike to clean when you get home.

Sometimes, rain is not a problem. A summer shower can be just the thing you need to cool you off. If you're already out and you have the right gear on, it's a minor inconvenience – you marvel at how good your new jacket is at shedding water, and just shrug and get on with it. But, if it rains heavily enough, summer or winter, then the ride becomes EPIC!!!

THE YORKSHIRE WORLD CHAMPIONSHIPS, SEPTEMBER 2019!!!

Life is full of those "well that didn't quite turn out how I imagined it" moments so, when a group of us decided in sunny May 2019 to ride over the border into Yorkshire to watch the cycling World Championships men's race later that year, none of us were picturing the Biblical scenes we'd be confronted with. (I've never understood this description as, given the length of The Good Book, it rains relatively little.)

September is usually quite a pleasant month in the UK (we got married in September – lovely day, it was, too) but, as the week approached, the country was being hit by a succession of storms, remnants of hurricanes brought over by the Gulf Stream. The World Championships time trials early on were badly affected but I thought, as I watched rider after rider slide across my tv screen, that this could not last until the weekend, surely?

We were due to leave on Saturday, staying overnight in Malham (about 35 miles from Harrogate), before riding over Sunday morning to watch the race roadside somewhere near the finish. Chances are that the sky would be all rained out by then.

Come the Saturday morning and Shelly dropped a slightly-less-than excited me off to rendezvous with Ged, Col, Andy and Martin in east Manchester. The rain had eased a little overnight but, the moment we slung our legs over our saddles, it began to pour again. We smiled grim smiles and set off on the sixty-something mile first leg of our journey.

The thing about riding in the rain is that the point comes, very quickly, when you realise that you're just going to have to put up with it. Happily, my coat held up pretty well, but the rest of me might as well have been sat in the puddles I was ploughing through. Every car and lorry that flew by might have brought further misery, but you can only get so wet so, while we were still on the move, it actually wasn't that bad.

The Theory of Cycling Relativity: Law 15
Rain will get in eventually - the only way to guarantee that you won't get wet is to stay indoors.

Conditions continued to worsen as we trekked upward into The Pennines, where brooks had burst their banks and found their way onto tarmac in their effort to find faster ways downhill. All talking had long ceased (bar the occasional "Oh, for f***'s sake!") and we battled on to our first stop in the lovely town of Hebden Bridge, which was around about halfway there. I had got cold coming down off the moors and so jumped at the chance of a window seat in a café just as the sun came out. There we steamed as we grabbed our second breakfast of the day. We all apologised for the puddles as we left.

We were fortunate that the sun stayed with us for the rest of the journey north (and that, bar the climb out of Hebden, it was generally downhill) and so, by the time we got to our destination of Malham, we were reasonably optimistic about the following day. The youth hostel where we were staying even had a drying room for our kit. Result!

Sunday, we awoke to rain. Within fifteen minutes of leaving Malham, we 'found' a puddle long enough and deep enough to saturate our feet and by the half-hour mark we were as wet as we'd been the previous day. We had decided to watch the race as it intersected with our route and then beat it back to Harrogate (the pros had a lot further to go) but, because the temperature had dropped a few degrees, the stop left me feeling too cold.

The race passed – half an hour late due to the weather and facing a further diversion – quickly, as it always does. Still, many in the peloton seemed to notice the snorkel and mask I was wearing for the occasion, which was nice. We remounted and set off for Harrogate. I was cold, wet, miserable, and riding into a headwind and rain that actually hurt. I cannot recall being so uncomfortable on a bike. I was so thoroughly fed up that, when I had the nagging feeling I'd left my phone on a wall back where we'd stopped, I decided that there was no way I was going back for it and I'd just have to get another. (As it turned out, it was safely in my rucksack.)

We arrived in Harrogate about forty minutes in front of the peloton and managed to get into town on the finishing circuit, which meant we had the great pleasure of being cheered on by the Dutch fans as we rode by. (They were great! We managed to get on a clip on YouTube, half-heartedly joining in the mad celebrations as we rode through the wall of techno music and bouncing bodies.) The plan to stop somewhere on the road to watch the riders go by was vetoed due to my near hypothermia and we ended up watching the race on television in a bar close to the finish line.

I got the train back to Manchester. It was still raining there.

HAIL

This is not the village in Leafy Cheshire where I used to have my shop (it's spelt differently, for a start), but the small, hard balls of ice that get thrown at you because a dark cloud has nothing better to do. It can happen at any time of the year, even on a bright, summer's day, and is all the more malicious because of it. If you're sufficiently covered, it makes a strangely satisfying tinkling sound on your helmet but, if you're out for that summer ride, suntan lotion is no defence and it hurts like hell.

Usually, it is hail's nature to be brief – it's the SAS of the meteorological world: come in, do the damage, and get out quickly – but sustained downpours can turn roads into rivers of ice with devastating effect, as happened in the 2019 Tour de France. I would like to advise "stop and stand under a tree" but, often, hail can be a precursor to or is joined by thunder and lightning, so don't stand under a tree, whatever you do. Do not think that your tyres will protect you from lightning – there is nowhere near enough rubber to provide insulation from a hit. Best advice, if you are unlucky enough to be caught in a lightning storm, is to get off your bike and find shelter under a bridge or in someone's house. Failing that, crouch somewhere well away from your bike, trees and telephone poles.

COLD

Cold, in itself, is not a problem. This is why layering was invented by the Ancient Greeks, who wore tunic over tunic over tunic on the days when they couldn't go around naked*. On most occasions, you will find that, having left the house in the appropriate garb, you will be more than adequately covered and might even be too hot. I've had so many mornings when I've overheated before reaching the front door that I now get dressed helmet first so as to keep my time in a centrally heated environment to a minimum.

I have a winter coat that I can only wear on THE COLDEST DAY SINCE RECORDS BEGAN! because it's so effective at keeping me warm. Either that, or wear nothing underneath, which would create problems should I need to take it off, say, at a coffee stop. I have a pair of gloves that are the same, the effect of both being to create so much sweat within ten minutes of riding that this then turns cold should I stop for even the briefest of moments, freezing me from the inside out. My wife uses the gloves whilst out with the dogs and I still wear the coat, but only if I'm doing anything less than a stroll.

[*This might not be true.]

Layering is the thing. I used to be a fishmonger, working first on outdoor markets and then, latterly, in an unheated shop. Things could get very cold and I quickly appreciated the advantages of layering clothes. The same goes for riding a bike (apart from the smell). Layering two or three thinner garments can keep you warmer than wearing one thicker one and you then have the option to take one or two off should the air temperature, or you, heat up.

Most of the time, we will have ample covering, but it is when cold is mixed with rain that things start to get uncomfortable. It doesn't even have to be that cold, either. The coldest I've been on a bike, was during a local sportive and the actual air temperature was well above freezing, but unforecast rain fell and turned my ride into a frozen hell. My fingers couldn't pull the brakes, my legs wouldn't work, and I was shaking so much my chain nearly unshipped. At one point, going up a small rise, I cramped in both legs at the same time and, physically unable to unclip, simply keeled over onto a grass verge. A couple of concerned riders who had stopped to ask if I was okay had to pick me and the bike up together and lean me against a tree until the cramp went away. Epic.

Cold, plus wet roads, means icy roads. Icy roads are bad. They can make your bike do all sorts of weird and wacky things, even when you are expecting it. Try not to ride on icy roads, because it might lead to unfortunate consequences (see "Accidents").

HEAT
Nothing says a summer ride like a fig roll nicely softened by back sweat.
Some people hate it, but I don't mind riding in hot weather. Usually, on even the hottest of days, you can temper the temperature by the breeze you create by moving forwards – it's the stopping that can be a problem. Much like having to get straight out of the house when fully

layered up against the cold, stopping on a really hot day can cause you to begin overheating (note: this is not "overeating", which is a different thing entirely). Overheating can go from being 'merely uncomfortable' to full-on heat exhaustion, which can cause anything from headaches to falling down unconscious, so it's not something you want to be putting up with for long.

Hot weather on the bike is all about staying cool and protecting yourself from the sun. Plenty of fluids and plenty of sunscreen is the way to go. And, if it's really hot, you could always take the odd break in the shade – this will help your body cool itself down. Remember all the sweat that is coming from inside you has to be replaced, so keep drinking. Think about that puddle of sweat beneath you when you've done a hard session on your turbo trainer: the same thing happens on a hot ride outside, only your puddle has disappeared into the atmosphere and onto the road. Drinks with electrolytes help to replace all the salty bits and pieces you drip out, so it's good, if you have two bottles, to have at least one of them so filled.

Life being life, though, even this drinking lark can be complicated, and you can in fact drink too much, inducing a condition called hyponatremia, which brings with it all manner of ills, from stomach cramps to short-term memory loss, to unconsciousness and coma (fun, eh?). So, keep taking a frequent swig, rather than necking down bottle after bottle. Like Goldilocks, you want to get it just right. The best way to check that you're on the right amount of fluids is by checking your urine. It should be the colour of pale straw (not the bendy ones you drink through): too much like clear water, you're drinking too much – too dark, you're not drinking enough. As I don't tend to need a pee whilst on the bike, I only get to find out how I'm drinking when I get home, which is a bit late. I find that sipping regularly and often does the trick. You really have to make a concerted effort to overdrink.

On sunny days, make sure you give yourself a good covering of sunscreen. Something sports related (waterproof/sweatproof), with a high SPF means that you can slap it on before you go out and be protected for the whole time you are out. If you are in for a particularly long day in the saddle, you may have to take a small tube with you to top up.

Check your jersey and shorts! Many pieces of summer-specific kit now come with built-in sun protection, but many do not, and it's all too easy to burn through the fabric. You won't feel it when you are enjoying your ride but, once you're back, you'll know about it! If in doubt, do a full body covering of sunscreen before you dress. If not, make sure to pay particular attention to areas like your nose, ears, back of the neck, backs of the legs and where your legs meet shorts and socks.

The great thing about warm days, especially if you are travelling somewhere to do a ride, is that all your kit – bar your shoes – will fit neatly inside your helmet! I've had winter rides where I've spent the night before laying out every single bit of cycle clothing I own and driven over to a mate's house with a holdall full of the stuff to then spend half an hour getting ready: this does not happen in hot weather.

THE FOUR SEASONS

Different seasons bring different weather, which is great for manufacturers of cycling apparel, but makes choices important in a pastime where you ideally do not want to be laden with gear you're not using.

Summer and winter are generally not a problem. Even in the UK, it's usually warm enough in summer to go out dressed minimally with a raincoat stuffed in your back pocket just in case. Winter means tights/leggings, gloves, and a coat that keeps you warm and dry. More often than not, you'll finish the ride wearing what you left home in. However, I have big issues with spring and autumn. There is no doubt that they are wonderful times of the year – whether leaves are greening the countryside or turning it to a rich russet – but they hugely increase my time stood in front of my cycling drawer. These are the times of the year when mornings that start cold might warm up...or not. Decisions have to be made. Do I wrap up and risk having to stow almost everything in three pockets that are already stuffed with mini pump, banana and fig rolls? Or do I gamble that it will warm up and freeze for (hopefully, only) the first hour of the ride? As I carry about as much fat as a carrot, I usually opt for more clothing, which means that the second halves of most rides have me feeling like a pack pony. I have rolled the dice and been lucky, but I have often lost and been chilled to the bone. It's also rather galling when, having borne the brunt of the early morning chill, you arrive home for the clouds to part. On one occasion, I got back following a particularly cold and wet (almost epic) time and had Shelly laughing at me as the sun came out and set me steaming as I cleaned my bike. I wasn't much in the mood to do something nice that afternoon, I can tell you.

You just have to embrace weather. As I pointed out at the beginning of this section, it is always there and, like hills, is just something to be surmounted. It might present you with a tough time on the bike, but it's very rare indeed that it can actually ruin a ride.

12. ON-BIKE NUTRITION

Food and drink are a hugely important part of riding a bike, particularly if you are out and about for more than an hour. The last thing you want to do is to run out of fuel. If you've had the misfortune to do so once, it's highly likely that you will have ensured that it is not something that will ever happen again.

On-bike feeding is a tricky business, especially if you don't wish to stop. (Pasta is a great source of carbohydrate fuel, but it does seem to always fly off the plate, particularly on tight corners.) As sugar is the easiest and simplest form of carb knocking about, most bars and gels available are sweet but, especially once you've eaten a few, these can turn out to be too sweet. Or too chewy: it's amazing how much harder it is to do the simple act of eating when you're on or near your limit, and this is generally when you need food the most. Best advice is to try different options on easier rides – the worst thing is to get halfway around a sportive and be at the point that you can no longer stomach the stuff that's filling your pockets – but, even then, you might find that they don't suit harder rides. Home-made options include jam sandwiches or rice cakes. Fig rolls, bananas and Bounty bars seem to be okay for me, then it's gels once I'm finding it tough to swallow solids. Even then, I've had occasions when my stomach has started to protest and send stuff back: there's only so much sweetness I can take. Sausage rolls would be great, but cold, they're too dry. (Cubes of cheese and pineapple on a cocktail stick would do the trick, but they do have that element of danger attached.) Most sportives will have food stops with less sweet alternatives available (cheese and ham sandwiches are always a great choice), and any longer weekend rides you do might be punctuated by a café stop. This is when you can, if you wish, get a savoury hit of eggs or beans or both on toast, washed down with, of course, coffee! Cake will usually be on the menu too.

Drinking on the bike is not just important when you are sweating buckets and it can be something that is easy to forget on the cooler days out. Get into the habit of taking a swig from your bottle frequently, whatever the weather. Cycling-specific drinks, like food, are commercially available, and can come in tablet or powder form, giving you many different flavours and all the added electrolytes you need. It's good to have at least one of your bidons filled with this stuff, rather than just plain water, as it provides an extra form of nutrition, especially if, like me, you have trouble getting food down on the bike.

It's also important to remember to fuel following a ride, particularly if it's been a tough one. Sometimes, no matter what you've tried to get down during the ride, you will still be running on empty, and something with a higher proportion of protein will be great at aiding post-ride recovery. There are plenty of flavoured recovery shakes on the market, but you can just as easily make your own with semi-skimmed milk and chocolate powder. I also like to chuck in an avocado or banana or dollop of peanut butter, or even, if I'm feeling outrageous, all three!

13. TO STOP OR NOT TO STOP

I'm a little bit ambivalent about café stops. This doesn't mean that I can eat cake with either right or left hand, but rather that I don't generally see the necessity to stop. It comes mainly from my history of riding alone when, if fig rolls have run out and the last gel has long since been sucked (this is what one does to gels, right?), the only option is to (epically) struggle on home. If ever I do stop, it's just to refill bottles. Usually, my lone rides are pretty meticulously planned, and I can be within fifteen minutes of my ETA, whatever their length. This means Shelly doesn't worry about me being dead somewhere because I'm always back when I said I'll be back. Café stops have the habit of throwing spanners into my near perfect timings and make her fret. I suppose I should call and tell her I'm going to be returning later than planned, but I'm usually enjoying myself far too much. In my defence, I do explain before I go that group ride lengths are unknowable and any return times I give her will be pure guesswork. (As well as the stops, group rides are subject to late arrivals, increased chance of mechanicals, and at least one of the group being on an off day: that I am even able to stipulate morning or afternoon return should be seen as a bonus.)

I never pause when riding solo, but pretty much every group ride we do is a café ride, the stop usually marking the halfway/turning point. The benefits of this are that I now don't have to cram my pockets full of bananas and fruity, biscuity things and we can stop for a chat – that jolly banter which is something that's sometimes hard to have on the move. Riding along, conversations are often hard to hear and constantly interrupted by traffic. Sitting around a table, with food and drink, gives us a time to catch up and, most importantly, take the piss*, that the cycling does not afford. Generally, we do not go into life's deep ponderables.

Upon arriving home, I'll often be questioned thus:
Shelly: What does he do for a living?
Me: Dunno.
Shelly: You're out for five hours with someone every Sunday and you don't know what they do???
Me: It's never come up. It's not important.
Shelly: So, what do you talk about?
Me: Oh, you know…stuff.
Shelly: Like what?
Me: Dunno, but it's funny.
Shelly: You're weird.

Obviously, the big thing about stopping at a café is the food. Much as I like fig rolls and flavoured water, they cannot hold a candle to a plate of eggs, beans and mushrooms – with, perhaps, a sausage or two - on toast, followed by strong coffee. Often, I will forgo the cake option because I need something savoury after all the sweet onboard fare. Having said that, flapjacks are great: if you get a good-sized one, you can eat half and stash the rest for a later onboard feed.

The problem with stopping at a café is the getting started again. If you're in a busy place, the pause in activity can be as long as an hour, if not longer, which is just the right amount of time for your legs to stiffen up nicely. On cold days, if you've not managed to snag a seat by a radiator, your personal dampness starts to overtake the heat you produced when riding which you are now not producing by sitting still. Then, putting cold, wet hat and gloves back on as you leave is not pleasant. As soon as you get out of the door, you feel a chill that was not there when you'd entered. This is not perfect preparation for the ride home.

I was once asked, whilst on a ride, whether I'd ever dropped in at a particular garden centre to make use of their on-site café. Said centre is less than a mile from my house. I pointed out that I couldn't comment on their carrot cake, but the birds in our garden are very happy with their seed mix.

[*I did look for an alternative phrase here, but could find anything that so accurately describes our conversations.]

14. WEIGHT

To be honest, unless you're a super-serious racer, needing to get down to your 5% body fat target, I don't think that worrying about your weight should be a big issue. For most of us, the simple act of getting out and riding will lead to an inevitable drop in waist size. Here's a bit of stuff I've learned and some of my own personal history…

Weight-loss diets work by cutting calorie intake, creating a deficit between calories taken in versus those expended. Many would-be dieters fail because they either find this too taxing and give up or, once they have achieved their goal, they think they've cracked it and go back to eating what they were eating before. To truly work, rather than a month off the beer and pizzas, a weight-loss programme has to be a lifestyle change. Cycling is a great way to lose weight because it is such a lifestyle change! Regularly riding your bike increases the calories you use and so hits one side of the balance and, given you are eating the same number of calories but expending more due to this prolonged exercise, you should see results reasonably quickly. Being fitter and lighter makes cycling easier and more enjoyable, so you're more likely to ride, which makes you fitter and lighter.

I've had three noticeable weight-loss moments in my life. During my twenties, alcohol, takeaways and fried breakfasts, and a more sedentary lifestyle, saw me hit thirteen stone. I was playing five-a-side football, squash and golf, but it was plain that the intake part of the calorie equation was far outweighing what I was expending. A change of job saw me ditch the breakfasts and I cut down on the pizzas and Chinese food (apologies, China) and I dropped a stone and a half so quickly that, when I went back to visit my old chums six months later, they thought I was ill.

When I was forty, I found the bike again. At this point, two-wheeled exercise was generally limited to two or three hours on a Sunday morning and nothing of any note during the week. Another six months down the line and I was down to eleven stone. Over the next couple of years, I maintained that weight but changed shape. I became leaner.

Then, aged forty-two, I gave up alcohol. This was due to a number of factors, the main one being that I felt I'd already had my lifetime's quota. Obviously, a lot of the stuff isn't great for you but, over the years, this hadn't stopped me. I never drank to get drunk, but I always seemed to end up that way and, the more it happened, the less I liked the way I felt. On a coach returning from a stag outing to York Races, I decided that enough was enough. We stopped off at a bar where someone bought a round of shots for the group. I declared that this was the last drink I would ever have, downed it, and phoned Shelly to come and pick me up. And that was that. Alcohol is full of empty calories: I shed another half stone and got down to where I am now, around 10st 7lb. Mentally, it wasn't easy to stop for good. I was very good at drinking and nobody believed I would keep my promise but, oddly, it was this that spurred me on. It turned the whole thing into a challenge, and I was determined to prove the doubters wrong.

All these were lifestyle choices rather than a sudden and brief wish to diet. The cycling helped because, in finding the bike, I found everything that went with it, and part of that came in the importance of what you eat. Pick up most cycling magazines and there will likely be one or two cycling-related recipes in there. Cycling's a healthy thing to do, so cycling-related recipes tend to be all about healthy food. It helped with me in that I tend to enjoy healthy stuff and don't see it as a chore to eat it. (Shelly would love to be the same but doesn't quite share my outlook: "I'd love to be a vegetarian, but I just don't like vegetables.") Yes, there's flapjacks and cakes to fuel the rides, but these are treats to be had on the bike and not off it. You don't really want to be going down the mental path of "Well, I've just ridden thirty miles, so I deserve a fry-up and eight cans of lager". This really defeats the object and you'll not drop too much weight with that view. You might even start adding to yourself.

There seems to be a point at which your own personal scale balances: when your cycling exercise no longer outweighs your calorie intake. This is natural for us mortals and it can be that trying to lose more weight will be detrimental to your ride. Since dropping to under eleven stone, my body composition has changed, even if my weight has not, so I'm much leaner and look thinner than I am (if that makes any sense). Mass lost from my upper body has been transferred to my legs. I could lose more weight by restricting my calorie intake, but the likely outcome would be that my body, still needing fuel to operate, would start to use that muscle. I could still ride, of course, but the chances are that I'd be soon at a point where performance is lost. It's a balancing act.

The Theory of Cycling Relativity: Law 16
Lighter can be better, but only up to a point.

In the two years that followed me closing the doors at my fishmongers, I naturally shed a bit of bulk from my upper body, largely due to the fact that I wasn't lugging large boxes of fish about anymore. It came to a point when, following a complete six week lay-off from any arm-related exercise due to my broken wrist, I was looking so thin up top that I was in danger of looking like a pro cyclist and, much as I'd like to ride like a pro, I don't want to look like one. I am not saying that pro cyclists are in any way unhealthy – far from it, in fact – but their body size and composition is structured and monitored by a team of sports scientists, dietitians and doctors. For the rest of us, getting down to something like their shape without proper supervision carries huge risks, especially if attempted too quickly. Don't try to look like somebody else, be the best shape for you.

If you're not careful, certain diets can adversely affect your performance. Watch out for any 'fad' diets. Take 'high protein–low carb'. These work in helping weight loss because protein tends to satisfy our hunger and fill us up more than carbohydrate, which always has a feeling of more, more, more. You'll take in fewer calories of protein and so lose weight. We also need protein to build muscle, so the more protein we eat, the more muscle we get.
Simple win-win, right?
The problem comes because we need carbohydrates for fuel. Simple carbs found in sugary, sticky stuff such as cakes and fruit are easy for the body to break down and use quickly. More complex carbs come in all the starchy, beige foods like bread and pasta. They release their energy more slowly. The good thing is that they are great sources of fuel during exercise – the drawback is that they are readily converted to fat and stored in the body if they're not used. (A moment on the lips, a lifetime on the hips!)

Like carbs, an excess of protein in the diet will be stored as fat. Exercising on a low-carb diet, the body will still need something to use for fuel and, devoid of carbohydrates will turn to readily available protein before fat because fat is, of the three, the slowest in its release of energy. The body's most readily available store of protein? Muscle.

So, you might well lose the weight, but that weight could be the muscle you want for pedalling, leaving you lighter but underpowered when you need it.

Actually, fat is our most efficient source of energy – it can supply around nine calories per gram, about twice that of carbs or protein – but it tends to get stored rather than used. Why? It seems that the body puts it away for when it is most urgently needed: it basically stores it for a rainy day. Oddly, fat stores can actually be accessed by very moderate exercise and, if you've heard about 'fat burning' and 'fasted rides', then this is what this is all about. The idea is to go out first thing in the morning and ride very, very easily. The body, which has yet to get any fuel in the form of carbs or protein, will access the fat stores. Because energy expenditure is so modest (if you're out of breath at any point you're really doing far too much), the body can rely on the slow release of fat energy. The trick is to keep it easy. A very long pre-breakfast walk can have a similar effect – so that easy.

Having said all this, you'll still only lose a tiny amount of weight (remember: it takes nine calories to use just one gram), and the best way to eat still seems to be a balanced diet with good, lean sources of protein, oily fish, plenty of fresh fruit and veg, nuts and seeds, and less of the stodgy fatty stuff. If you are intent on losing weight, you should try to lose it as slowly as possible. If you're relatively happy with your diet and don't see the need to change it, just drop the portion sizes slightly. Worried you might still be hungry? Have a glass of water before each meal – it will make you feel full (and many of us don't drink enough during the day, anyway). The worst thing is to try and shed the pounds quickly. Overdoing the weight loss will soon bring you to the point where there are days where you just don't feel like going out for a ride, and that's not really the result you want, is it?

Like many things, weight can only be an issue if you make it one. I never set out to lose weight, it was just a side effect of my lifestyle change. Other people notice it more than I do, and I only ever weigh myself if I have to work out power to weight ratios*, or fill in a form. Usually, if you get out on a bike – or do any daily exercise routine - the weight loss should start to take care of itself. For most recreational cyclists starting out, the thing that's making life difficult is not necessarily their weight, but the fact that their legs are suddenly doing a job they've never done before (or for a very long time). Repetitive cycling will strengthen leg muscles that aren't used to pedalling and each future journey should be that bit easier: the trick in the early days is not to give up before you've given it a good chance.

It is also entirely possible that you might not lose weight at all by riding a bike but then, if that's the reason you're cycling, I think that you're missing the point.

[*To get this, divide your FTP power by your weight in kilos. Mine works out at just over 4 (but, with good looks and charisma, that equates to about 7 on the road). It's another balance – a score moveable by tipping one of the sides – so you can increase your power to weight number either by gaining power or by losing weight whilst keeping that power.]

July 4th-8th 2016
"When are you going to ride it?"
We've only just unpacked. It's been a long journey so, first of all, I need to let my back loosen up, and then I have to do some riding. I can't just rock up and ride it.

So, every day before breakfast, I'm out for a ride. It's never too long. Along the valley to Montbrun, up and over to Sault and back, or down the other way and up that steep road to Brantes and over the Col des Aires. Nothing too taxing, but always with a bit of climbing involved. Sometimes, the day ends with a ride, too. Shelly has brought her bike, and that Montbrun road is generally good, reasonably quiet and, importantly for her, mostly flat.

In my mind, 'easy does it' is the way to go. I've been riding harder all year to be ready for this and, even if I say so myself, I'm in pretty good shape. All I need is to keep the legs moving until I decide to make the climb.

Later in the week, I receive a tweet from cycling journo Daniel Freibe suggesting, as a warm-up, I take on the Montagne De Lure. A cycling journalist and on the spot cycling interviewer (one of the more famous hand/mic combos in the business), and writer of cycling books including two about big hills, he knows his stuff, so it's advice I'm more than happy to take on board. A climb of just under 1,300m over 24km, with an average of around 6%, it is topped with a red and white mast. It's like Ventoux's little brother! Added to that, it's on the way to

Sisteron, so we can do some sightseeing in the afternoon.

So, on Friday morning, we turn right off the D946 a few miles outside of town and stop on the D53, a narrow road which seems, at first glance, to be going between two mountains rather than up one. Shelly drops me and the bike off at the junction and leaves me to make her own way up to the top in the car. It's still early, but already hot as I spin along through fields in the shallow valley for a couple of kilometres. There's a scattering of houses, but no-one about. It's all very pleasant, but I know from experience that the flat bits bring the average gradient down and the longer the easy flats, the more I will have to pay later on.

Soon enough, the fields give way to light woodland and I bear right, over a bridge where, wonderfully, a fox lies sunning itself. I look at it, it looks at me. I cycle on, it carries on sunbathing. From here, as the wood becomes forest, the road begins to gradually ramp up as it traverses the lower slopes of the mountain. One thing I've noticed about climbing through trees is that it robs me of all perception of gradient. I know I'm working hard but the trees rob me of picking out a viewpoint to define my slope. My computer doesn't show gradient, so all I have to rely on are the frequent roadside markers which count down my way to the summit and tell me how high I've come and how steep the road is. Oddly, they do not mark exact kilometres, and count down 13.2, 12.2, 11.2, etc.*

I pass a flattened snake and mentally remark on what poor luck it must have had to be run over on a road where, as yet, the only other living soul I've seen has been a fox. Now and again, the trees break, and I can see to my right how high I have come.
Then, the traverse ends and I'm into a series of long hairpins. Higher now and, looking northeast, I can see, in the not too far distance, the Alps! It's tough going as the heat is quite oppressive and there's little breeze. Sweat covering my sunglasses has clouded my view to such an extent that I now have to take them off, but I can't get them quickly slotted into my helmet and nearly ride off the road trying. I'm still grinding out a regular rhythm, but it's not quite fast enough to get rid of the column of flies that have joined me. I see a couple of riders up ahead, all mountain bikes and backpacks – God, they must be hot – and get out of my saddle to sprint past them (with a cheery "Bonjour", obviously). Luckily, I lose many of my tiny companions in the effort.
The road cuts out of the trees and switches to the right, over a rise, to take me onto the other side of the mountain. This is the Pas de la Graille, and the views from here are just breathtaking. I'm not stopping, though, and am spilled out onto low deciduous wood and alpine meadow, quite different to the deep mixed forest of the road I've just climbed, across which to the west, I can make out The Bald Mountain itself. The road flattens out and I notice the marker telling me 1.1km to go (I must have lost 100m

somewhere down the mountain). I can see Shelly now, parked up on a flat bit at the top and, at the 0.1km marker, I get out of the saddle once more to put on a show for the camera.

The only other person up there is an old fellow in a VW Campervan. Shelly's a little unsure what his reaction will be but that doesn't stop me celebrating the moment by getting naked and standing like Christ the Redeemer at the summit.

Sisteron's very nice.

Right, I'll do Ventoux on Monday.

[*I should really find out why.]

15. SPORTIVES

It was training for and taking part in a sportive with a friend that got me back into cycling. Although I was looking forward to the event, other than the fact it was fifty miles long, I didn't really know what to expect. We spent most Sunday mornings during the summer doing easy rides of around twenty to thirty miles and then, somewhat quickly, September arrived, and it was time to do The Ride. We turned up to a park bustling with bikes and their riders, stood nervously in the queue for the start, and then, with the pings of cycling computers going off all around us, we were away.

Riding in a large group was another first, but we made our way excitedly up through our bunch and were quickly riding out of town and heading for the countryside. Too quickly for me, as it turned out. After five miles, I had blown. The course was not particularly mountainous – the longest climb was probably no more than a mile – but nor was it flat, and the constant change in gradient made it an incredibly tough and long forty-five miles. I learned a lot that day.

Here are some things to think about if you're considering taking part in a sportive:

1. Sportives are hugely popular events and are generally attended by a wide spectrum of the cycling fraternity, from the under-prepared guys in football shorts and backpacks on their mountain bikes right through to the speed freaks

on time trial machines. Most events offer a choice of route length, but it pays to check out the terrain first. I've seen a middle-aged couple standing roadside in tears because they had underestimated their day. That sportive started and finished in Chester – which is flat – but they failed to realise that the bits in between were through the Welsh borders – which is most definitely not flat. They were halfway round and it was as hard to go back the way they had come as it was going to be to ride on. It was not the jolly day out they had planned. I wonder if they're still there…
So, it's important to do your research, because one fifty miler might be twice as hard as another.

2. Pace yourself! Because there are a wide range of abilities on the road, it's all too easy to fall into the trap of trying to hold the wheel of someone who is streets ahead of you (literally). Go too fast too soon and, as I found to my cost on my first sportive, it won't take long for you to run out of steam. This is especially true when riding up hills. Although you might want to post a good time, ride within your limits and don't get dispirited if riders pass you. Do your own thing. On that Chester sportive, I was mortified at one point as quite a few riders passed me on the early slopes of the Horseshoe Pass out of the Welsh town of Llangollen. It's a climb about 4 miles long, averaging 5%. I am, let's not forget, "The Flying Goat of Leafy Cheshire (Scourge of All Inclines)!" so it was a bit odd to feel myself going backwards as the road began to rise. I

didn't panic, though, and carried on tapping out my own pace. It actually turned out to be a massive psychological boost on what was quite a tough ride as, one by one, I reeled them in and overtook them on my way to the summit.

The Theory of Cycling Relativity: Law 17
The quietest thing in the world is a group of cyclists struggling up a hard climb.

On another sportive, I noticed one year that I was riding up my nemesis, Winnats Pass, at little more than walking pace, and arriving at the top truly knackered. I decided then, that the following year, I would try walking up. The energy I would save, I surmised, would more than make up for any time lost. On the day, as the pass loomed ahead, I resolved to stick to my plan, although I made sure that I was still aboard and dancing on the pedals like Contador in his pomp as I passed the official photographer on the lower slopes. Then I hopped off, took off my shoes (it's not easy walking up 20% inclines in cleats) and walked to the top. There, I climbed back on and rode past a large group of cyclists who had, to their credit, pedalled all the way up, but were now paying for it. My plan worked perfectly, and I ended the sportive having taken ten minutes off the previous year's time.

3. Many of the sportives I have taken part in have had their start-finish at a racecourse or the

local county show grounds. If you are driving to the start, arrive in good time as it can take a while, particularly if it's a popular and well attended ride, to get parked. It's also highly likely that, even in summer, you'll then have to walk through wet grass to sign in. I always turn up in walking boots or wellies. I may look a little odd with the rest of my cycling kit on, but at least I'll have dry feet for the start. Another top tip is to take your own toilet paper. The cubicles are always busy pre-ride, the queues can be long, and it can be a bit of a depressing start to the day if you're on the wrong end of a shortage.

4. Most sportives will have food stops but it's better to take something of your own along anyway. Obviously, it's handy not to have to stuff your pockets with grub at the outset but, you never know, you might get to the first stop and discover that there's little there that you can stomach or simply little there. Some sportives are not as amply stocked as others. Rather than relying on the on-course cuisine, you can use it as a top-up service.

Having said this, they are there for good reason so, even if it's just to refill your bottles and stretch your legs and back for a minute or two, it's often beneficial to stop.

The Theory of Cycling Relativity: Law 18
Stopping during a ride can often lead to a faster result.

Whether you pause or not, do not forget to keep eating and drinking.

5. It's highly likely that you'll be setting off early in the morning and out on the road for up to five or six hours on some longer routes. Even during the summer, this can mean a cool start and, even if it's sunny, there's always the chance of rain, so don't underdress! If you're driving to the start, take more than you think you'll need, as it gives you the option of making a choice when you arrive there, and you can always leave gear you don't wear in the boot. Layers can be taken off if need be, and a packable raincoat stowed in a pocket is always a useful addition to a cyclist's wardrobe. I learned the hard way during one Epic! sportive in October and now, unless we're in the middle of a heatwave, I always have a coat with me.

6. It may sound an obvious one, but remember to carry spare tubes, levers, tool etc.

7. Find some friends. If you are riding alone, it helps to join a group. That fact about saving 40% of effort by riding behind others is not lost on the pros, so why not use it yourself? Starts are usually staggered, so you will usually find yourself as part of a large group for the first few miles anyway. The trick, then, is to seek out others who are riding at your pace and stick with them. Make sure that you take your turn on the front (see "Etiquette", later on) and, by cooperating, a difficult route can be made that bit

easier. I once found myself alone and riding into a headwind on a sportive from Carlisle up into Scotland and back. Looking behind, I spotted a group of four, so I waited and latched on as they came by. I had been riding solo for four or five miles at around 17mph: as a group, we completed the final forty miles at over 20mph. There was even one point where, as the last man in the group at a turn off, I was cut adrift by oncoming traffic, but the rest of the group waited as they saw the advantage in having that extra pair of legs (and they obviously knew talent when they saw it).

The problem is not necessarily finding the group, but keeping it together. As sportives are generally a mass of differing abilities, groups will tend to fracture on the first hill. That Carlisle ride has proven to be the exception rather than the rule and it's usually the case that, especially if there are a number of hills early on, groups are quickly fractured. After a while, the sportive is a line of individuals strung out as far as the eye can see. There is a coming together at feed stops, of course, but it tends to be the case that riders come in in dribs and drabs, and then leave the same way. The great majority of sportives I've taken part in, I've ridden most of the routes alone.

8. This is something I briefly alluded to in point 2. Pretty much every sportive has an official photographer, so keep an eye out. If you do want a memento of the occasion, other than a bottle of water and a tacky finisher's medal, you

want to be looking good in it. Look out for the guy crouching by the side of the road and get in your best pro position for the photo: aero tuck for downhill and dancing on the pedals on a climb works. Often, there are two or more locations, so you can always have a super serious one in one place and a funny, wave at the camera shot in another. Try to ensure there's no snot dripping from your nose.

I am normally very successful in this but, on one occasion, I had an epic fail. The Cheshire Cat sportive takes in, as part of its route, the dreaded Mow Cop. Now, I've ridden up it many times and, tough though it is, I have never had any problem. This time, the ride out from the start in Crewe was into a headwind and near horizontal rain so, although it came relatively early (about 15 miles) into the ride, many cyclists were knackered by the time they'd reached the bottom of the climb. Since it was the first hill with a relatively flat run in, there were still lots of us on the road together, and so I had to pick my way through and around others as we began. I knew, from previous experience, that the photographer would be perched on the final 25% stretch. I rode conservatively up the lower slopes, so I'd be ready to dance on the pedals for the camera. As I neared the top, I got stuck behind another rider who was weaving all over the road in his effort to make headway. I moved to the right to go around, but he kept going that way too, and I was forced so far over that I ran out of road. I ended up clipping the kerb and down I went on my backside. Right in front of the photographer. As I went, I heard click-click-click-click-click.

I propped myself up on my elbow. "Did you get that?"

"Oh, yes!" he said, as he gleefully took another.

The gradient there was so steep that it would have been a nightmare to try and clip back in to continue up the final fifty yards or so, so I either had to ride back down to the bottom and begin again, or pick up my bike and walk the rest of the way to the top. I picked up my bike and began to walk the rest of the way to the top. I discovered, when I went on his website a couple of days later, that he'd got pictures of that moment too. I didn't buy any.

8(a). Don't forget the finish line celebration. There will likely be a camera there, too. No matter how hard it's been or how tired you are, look like you've won the thing!

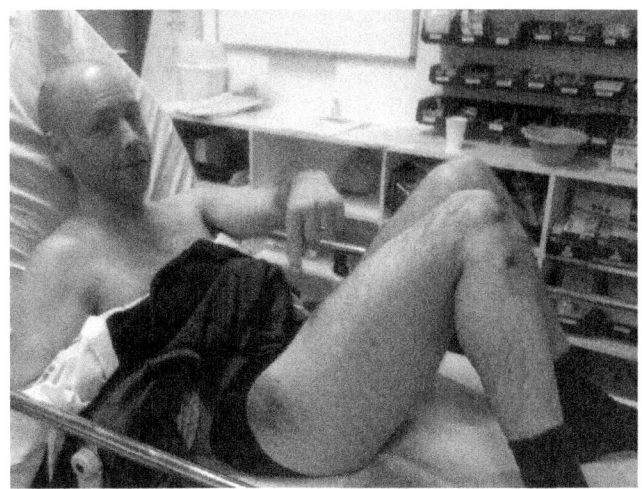
Cycling is fun! My first cycling-inspired visit to hospital, for a broken collar bone and assorted grazes. I was such a brave little boy. (Note the hairy legs: I had yet to start shaving.)

Always pose for the cameraman. Banishing the memory of that first sportive by returning and taking an hour and a half off my time. Pacing was the key. And food. But mainly pacing.

Can we pick 'em? The view from the cottage across to Bealach-Na-Ba. Awesome, but it gave me the willies every morning.

Nearly at the top of a ride I enjoyed going up far more than going down…and the going up was tough.

EPIC!!! Leaving Malham Youth Hostel with the lads on day 2 of our trip to the 2019 World Championships, and it's already raining. We weren't smiling for long.

Be prepared! Waiting for the Worlds peloton to come by. It rained. A lot. (Note Ged in the background with the arrow he always brings with him so we don't lose him.)

There has to be balance in life and (apart from Shelly, obviously) the dogs are my other great love. Admittedly, that balance is still somewhat tipped towards cycling.

On-bike nutrition is important. Bagels are great for taking on a ride, and they fit perfectly on the bike!

On the Champs Élysées, July 21st 2013, for the Tour's finale. It's 10.30am and, having found an ideal spot, Shelly settles down to wait.

A mere eight and a half hours later, and the peloton arrives!

Always stay hydrated. Relaxing after a particularly hot ride around Leafy Cheshire.

What a view! Celebrating scaling Montagne De Lure, a warm-up for Ventoux. I was under strict instructions that there was to be no repeating this atop the Bald Mountain.

The Flying Goat of Leafy Cheshire is nearly there.

"Yeah!"
Just, "Yeah!"

16. THE HOLIDAY PROBLEM*

[*As I write this I am sitting on a Cretan beach. All the sun-loungers, except one, face the sea. Mine is facing inland to the mountains, where I can see a road snaking steeply upwards. "Hmm, I wonder where that's going…"]

Life can be fraught with logistical difficulties when not everybody in the household is onboard with one's cycling passion. Holidays can be a huge problem because a holiday might mean two whole weeks without riding your bike and, given that you ride your bike for (a) exercise and (b) relaxation, what might be a stress-free time in the hot sun to others could be exactly the opposite for you. There's every chance that you won't be allowed to take your kit and wear it around the pool (just in case there's bike hire) so you'll spend your time worrying about losing your carefully cultured cycling tan lines. While the rest of the clan are chilling out, you'll be watching your thighs wither away and turn from hard-earned mighty tree trunks into two thin strands of (admittedly, wholemeal) spaghetti.

Thankfully, our tans do mark us out so it's quite easy to spot another cyclist on an enforced break – they'll usually have a Merckx or Coppi biography to help them cope, and will gaze wistfully at pedalos – and you can form a little support group to get through cycling cold turkey. Often, a knowing nod or sly cyclist's wave is enough to signal that there is someone else who's feeling your pain. It's nice to know that there's another who is in the same boat of not being on a bike.

But what happens when you have a non-cycling partner and want to go away and take the bike with you? Given that you're riding most of the time, how are you going to approach the subject? The answer is 'carefully'...

"BEALACH-NA-BA!"
It is January 2015, and I have decided that I want to ride up Bealach-Na-Ba, in the north-west of Scotland. The problem facing me, apart from the apparent difficulty of the climb itself, is that it is not an easy place to get to. It's certainly not somewhere I could ride out to of a Sunday morning from my leafy Cheshire abode. Even if I drove halfway and dumped the car, I'd still not be back in time for tea.
What I needed was a plan.
I couldn't tell Shelly I was off up to the far north west of the isles just to ride up one hill. But I might – I just might – get away with it if I hid the ride inside a holiday. It had to be carefully done, though.
"Shelly, fancy going to Scotland this year?"
"That would be nice." And I was off!
Now, most of our holidays, especially those in this country, are booked in the following manner: I pick the location, and Shelly picks accommodation. It's worked out this way because I'm good at finding wonderful

surroundings, but I don't really care where I rest my head once I'm there. She demands quite a high minimum level of comfort, but her geographical knowledge is awful – as bad as her understanding of the history and political intrigues of the Middle East.

This allows me a certain freedom of choice. (It's also why we seldom discuss the Middle East.)

"Where shall we go then?" she asked.

"I believe the Applecross Peninsula is simply breath-taking."

"Oh, where's that?"

"Just above Skye."

"But we've been to Skye."

A tricky moment, "We haven't been just above Skye though."

"No. You're right." Averted!

Her eyebrows were raised once or twice along the way, as I seemed rather more insistent on a tighter search radius than in previous holidays. It's hard enough to find decent lodgings having two dogs in tow, and pickings were slim in one of the least populated areas of the country.

I kept her in the dark as long as I could, but there would come a point that I'd have to tell her – it would look a bit odd me packing the bike otherwise.

So, eventually, we settled on a wonderful cottage in a tiny place called Achintraid, which happened to be on the banks of Loch Kishorn.

Amazingly, it was directly across the loch from Bealach-Na-Ba!

"Amazingly, it's directly across the loch from Bealach-Na-Ba!" I said.

"Who, or what is that?"

"Oh, it's just quite a famous hill that people sometimes cycle up."

Silence.

"I might take my bike, if that's okay?"

More silence, and then: "Fine, but you're not disappearing every bloody day. I'm not having this holiday hijacked by cycling."

(Too late.)

The blow was softened somewhat when I suggested that she could take her bike, too. "We could go for romantic evening spins along the loch!" That she only ever rides in warm sunshine, and the trip was planned for September, when the weather would be, at best, 'changeable' meant that these spins might turn out to be ever so fleeting, but she seemed happy enough to go along with it.

In the intervening months, I attempted to pique her interest with numerous articles about the pass. Lots of pictures of the area. And maps! But she showed little enthusiasm.

"What am I looking at?"

"A map of the area!"

"Why?"

"So you can see where we're going."

"Won't I see it when we get there?"

(Shelly does not, like me, value the beauty of an Ordnance Survey map: she is left cold by contour lines and shrugs at the mere mention of a tumulus or trig point. When she's discovered me spending time gazing at maps as things of awe and wonder, she's told me to stop being so odd.)

It was only when we did get there, after an eight-hour journey – two stops to let the dogs out and one massive argument about petrol prices in Fort William (who knew it would be one pence cheaper half a mile down the road?) – that she appreciated that (a) it was a stunningly beautiful part of the world, and (b) it was quite a steep road up and over that mountain over there on the other side of the loch.

Now we'd gone all that way, Shelly just wanted me to get the climb out of the way, so we could get on and enjoy the holiday. But it's not that easy, is it? Every morning, for almost the full week, I watched the tiny dots that were mostly campervans crawl up the thin ribbon of road, clinging to what seemed to be the sheer side of a cliff, and disappear into the cloud.

I came up with excuse after excuse: back's hurting after the long drive; it's too cloudy, too windy; even though it's sunny here, it's raining over there. To be fair, these were all valid points. I was waiting for the perfect weather, which is not a common occurrence, especially in Scotland, but she wanted the ride over and done with – literally. After all, there was more to the holiday than bloody cycling!

As the end of the week approached, I still hadn't ridden the climb. Then, on Thursday, like The Simpsons intro, the clouds miraculously parted. I rode the mile or so around the loch to turn off the main road at Tornapress and, as Shelly drove on ahead, I rode the climb.

For anyone who's not done it and wants to: the first bit's pretty easy as you ride gently upward along the road above the river to where it empties into the loch and round a bend to cross a valley. It's this benign start that brings the average gradient of the climb down to 7%. It's not until you've traversed this neighbour, then crossed over a bridge and rounded the headland and into the gates of hell that the climb proper and the real hurting begins. From here on, it's 9% and 10%, rearing up to 20% on occasions.

It's a single-track road, so go when it's likely to be quieter, or else you'll be stopping all the way up to let motor vehicles past. The decidedly rural surface and the constant threat of meeting sightseeing cars and vans coming around blind bends towards you means that the ride back down is far less fun than it should be. There are, I believe, some wonderful views to be had from the top, over the bay to Raasay, Rona, and Skye. I didn't see them as, by the time I reached the top, the clouds and rain had returned. Top tip: take a coat.

As it turned out, we did go for romantic spins along the loch, and Shelly actually came with me as I re-rode the easy first part of the climb up to the little bridge. And she even sort of enjoyed it!

On the eight-hour long drive back south (it's no quicker just because it's downhill) it struck me that the Tour had not visited Ventoux for a couple of years. Flushed with success, I felt it was well worth taking a chance.

"Fancy a fortnight in Provence next July?"

17. ACCIDENTS

Accidents happen – it's a fact of life – but, when accidents happen on your bike it does tend to hurt a bit more than a paper cut, or even banging your head on a toilet seat and nearly knocking yourself out whilst endeavouring to tie a shoelace (don't ask). Watch any pro race and you're more than likely to see someone hit the deck. More often than not, they'll get straight up, ripped and bloodied perhaps, get another bike thrust into their hands, and off they go, pausing momentarily to clip their computers and feet in. Sometimes, they'll sit in the middle of the road like a bewildered sparrow and, if they're gingerly cradling an arm, you can nod sagely and say to yourself "collarbone". Sometimes, just sometimes, they don't get up.

As we're doing much the same thing as them, at an admittedly slower pace, we mere mortals are up against the same fates as the pros. Cycling can be fun. Cycling can be exciting and exhilarating. But cycling can be tough, and it is not safe.

Since I've been back on the bike, I've hit the deck badly three times. Each time, the fall did not involve another cyclist or vehicle: all were due to road conditions. Bizarrely, during my first incarnation as a cyclist – ages 4 to 16 – I cannot recall a single serious incident. I did some ridiculously stupid things on two wheels during those years, usually as part of one dare or another, and came through in one piece. The one time I did fall off, I would have been about five years old, and came off at the bottom of The Cobbles. I still remember the single trickle of blood from my knee down my leg and into my sock. I went running home to my dad, who told me off for not properly pronouncing the Ts in the phrase "It hurts." (No mental scar there, then!) Other than that, I managed to avoid any sort of tarmac-related incident.

The first time I came down heavily was in 2011, within just two years of riding again. I was descending a hill, fully in control and not too fast and, whilst checking out an upcoming bend for oncoming traffic, I rode over a depression in the road which I'd missed due to shadow. The bike dropped from under me and I bounced out of the saddle.

The next thing I knew, I was sitting in the middle of the road, a considerable distance down the hill from where I had been, like a bewildered sparrow, and cradling my right arm (you can nod sagely now, if you like).

I checked the bike, which was fine (yay!), and then I called Shelly:

"Hey babe, can you come and pick me up? I've come off and broken my collarbone."

"How do you know?"

"It's in two pieces."

"Oh God!" She didn't once ask about the bike, but I put that down to shock.

At the hospital, I was triaged by a nurse who was also a cyclist. She nodded sagely when I told her what had happened, "Hmm, like a bewildered sparrow, you say?"

Now, usually in these circumstances, it is the medic who wants to cut off the expensive merino base layer while the patient objects and frantically fights to keep it in one piece. After all, that and my shoes and socks were the only bits of clothing I hadn't trashed in the fall. Here, we had the situation of a sympathetic nurse trying her best to save me some money.

"Oh, that's a nice base layer. Let's see if we can get it off over your head."

"No, it's okay," I said, "I don't think I can lift my arm enough."

"But if we just…"

I had to give her some credit, she tried her best but, after the fourth time and I screamed "Just cut the fucking thing off!" she came around to my way of thinking.

I could see that she felt she'd failed.

They kept me in just long enough for Shelly to pop out to the local Tesco to get me a set of pyjamas, and then decided to send me home. The collarbone will heal itself, they said, so no need for an operation to pin it. And it did, only it means that my right shoulder is now a couple of inches narrower than my left and this has led to problems on the bike as I'm now a bit lopsided. On the upside, should I need to, I can now follow cats through holes in fences!

My second chute came at the end of a long skid which came at the end of a long, wet hill. When your brakes lock and you start to slide, you're supposed to ease off and let the bike roll on, but I was rapidly heading for a T-junction and so did not have that option. I managed to hold it, hold it, hold it, and then the back wheel flipped the other way, and we parted company. I took the final twenty metres of the slope on my side and back. The guy riding behind me told me he'd wished he had a GoPro because it was most impressive! For me, it was another pair of ripped shorts and jacket, and big holes in my thigh, elbow and wrist. The bike was fine, though (yay!).

The Theory of Cycling Relativity: Law 19
Accidents can be as painful to the pocket as they are to the body. On the plus side, they often result in upgrades.*

[*this is not a good reason to have an accident!]

I still had thirty miles to ride back. As there was nothing, apart from a bit of pride, broken, my phone call home this time was just to check that we had enough bandages and plasters. I never have a reason to call when I'm out on a ride so for her to hear my ringtone would undoubtedly have made her anxious. That, at the exact moment that Shelly answered, an ambulance went past me, sirens blaring, did not help allay her fears. One of us found that quite funny. The other let him know how unfunny it was while she

was splashing on the antiseptic when he got home.
I got a few wide-eyed looks through car windows as I made my way back, battered and bloodied. At the time, I thought it looked far worse than it was…but that was before the pain came.

Sometimes, accidents are just plain embarrassing. On one sportive, I rode into the car park where the food stop was unaware that the puddle at the entrance was hiding a bit of a hole. It was quite a small area, so many cyclists were gathered round as I swept through the gate, came to an abrupt halt, and went head-first over my handlebars. Fortunately, the only thing that was hurt was my pride and, as luck would have it, the sudden deceleration made all the snot shoot out of my nose and cleared me out for the rest of the ride. Bonus!

"I TOLD YOU NOT TO GO OUT!"
Most recently, I have been left, from a cycling point of view, housebound with a broken wrist. This came courtesy of my need to be riding outside.
Early January is rarely the best time of the year to ride and this year was no different. The usual snow hadn't appeared but had been replaced by weeks of wind and rain. When, eventually, there was a break in the weather – and it was at on a weekend! – I decided that I must seize my chance. The only problem, a minor one from my point of view, was that the break in rain was due to a cold snap.

"Don't go out today." said Shelly. "Why don't you go on your turbo trainer?"
"I need to ride outside." I replied, and I was right, I did.
"Well, be careful."
As if I wasn't going to be careful!
The early part of the ride was fine. I was well aware that there could be some hairy moments ahead, but the day before had been dry and I guessed that any black ice would have disappeared then. In any case, I was keeping to main roads, where motor traffic would have worn away any danger.
I was just out to get some miles in, and just to be outside. I wasn't going 'head down/full gas' but it was bloody cold, so I was going as fast as the conditions would allow. And all was well until about five miles in. I turned left, onto another road, and, in doing so, must have taken a line closer to the edge that all the cars had missed. I hit black ice. The bike slid from under me, and down I went. It's always an odd moment as you immediately comprehend what is happening but realise there's not a lot you can do about it and so prepare for impact.
It must have been a particularly slippery bit of road because the bike did a complete one-eighty beneath me and I ended up on top of the handlebars. Because it had simply slipped away, I had dropped like a stone and face-planted. Fortunately, the top half of me had fallen onto the grass verge so, rather than ruining my dashing good looks, I was left picking grass, soil and ice out of my mouth and nose. My left wrist

hurt a bit and I was winded. A car stopped and the driver asked if I was okay. I told him I was fine (I wasn't) and checked the bike. No damage there (yay!). I checked my kit – no damage there, either. All good… apart from my wrist.

Now, straight away I should have turned around and gone home, but I'd only just left the house, so on I rode, nursing the wrist but assuming it would get better as I went. I was out for another hour. The only reason I didn't stay out longer was that the wrist was preventing me riding hard and, because of that, I was getting steadily colder. I had formed a layer of ice where the sweat had wicked through to the surface of my jersey and frozen. Pedestrians were giving me funny looks. I needed to get home.

I arrived home to an empty house as Shelly was still out with the dogs, so I stood in the kitchen, in my puddle of meltwater, and waited for her to get back. The pain in my wrist was now such that I couldn't even take my gloves off, let alone the rest of my gear, so I calmly remained in the same spot, semi transfixed by the increasing pond at my feet.

When, ten long minutes after I'd arrived home, she returned, I took a leaf out of the dogs' playbook and held out my paw.

"I told you not to go out!"

"It'll be fine." I said. "It hurts a bit now, but it will be fine."

I, of course did not go straight to the hospital as there was football and then snooker on the television – priorities, right? – and I was still certain that everything would be better the

following day. I spent the night propped up on and fighting the dogs for room on the sofa.
The following day, at the hospital, the X-ray showed a double fracture of the radius.
All of my friends (for once) agreed with my wife.
'Dickhead' seemed to be a common term. And dickhead was right, because, whilst seeking to sneak in an hour or two of extra cycling, I had effectively taken myself off the road for six weeks. I had forgotten:

The Theory of Cycling Relativity: Law 6
Sometimes, it's better not to ride.

As well as the holes in your skin, your kit, and, subsequently, your pocket, accidents do not help your riding immediately after. Remember TToCR: Law 10? Confidence is a big thing, from actually winning that battle as a kid to move along on just two wheels, to staying upright on them for the rest of your life. Accidents have a habit of knocking confidence that spoils your future enjoyment, but only for as long as you let it. It's a natural thing – it makes perfect sense for our brains to tell us to avoid anything that has previously done us harm – but it is something that you need to override rather than avoid. The longer you leave it, the more excuses you find, the harder it will be to get back out on the road.

A SHORT NOTE ON HELMETS
Wearing one, if it isn't mandatory, is a completely personal thing and I know that

arguing for or against can be divisive. I will say only this:

Both times I came off, my head hit the deck. The first time, I hit the road so hard that I actually broke my helmet and, since I don't actually remember the moment of impact (as I do during the second fall) it is entirely possible that I was knocked unconscious. I am much happier that it was a broken helmet and not a broken head. Here endeth the lesson.

FAILURE TO UNCLIP

A (usually) much less painful, but far more embarrassing, rite of passage is failure to unclip.

To many of us of who spent our early days riding around on flat ones, clipless pedals (oddly, these are the ones you clip in and out of) can come as a bit of a shock. Whilst offering far more efficiency during the 'riding around' bit of riding, they can take some getting used to when you have to stop. Now, it is not a case of simply taking your foot off the pedal as it is fixed into place: you have to remember this and be ready to twist out and unclip your foot and get it down before balance is lost. Often, a sudden stop, or indecision over whether to stop or carry on, or even which foot to put down, can lead to catastrophe as the cosmic balance window closes. Brain freeze on how the whole system works will bring on disaster as you forget what you are supposed to do, panic, and end up doing nothing. It is not unlike when, whilst learning to drive a car, you might stall the engine at a junction. The only difference is that, sat in the car, there is far less chance you'll keel over onto the road.

It can take only a moment but seems to happen in slow motion. The best thing to do is to brace for impact and hope that not too many people are looking, although, since it usually happens at junctions it means that, sadly, you are always likely to have an audience.

It happened to me a couple of times within weeks of me setting off on my clipless voyage.

On the first occasion, I was most fortunate to have come to a stop next to a tree and I toppled in that direction, so I came to rest still reasonably vertical. A few days later, I was not so lucky and came to grief at a busy junction in the centre of a village. I swear, from nowhere, there was a ripple of applause. Much as I am aware of how funny it looked – a little like being gently knocked over by an invisible bowling ball – I did not hang around to do an encore.

So, the thing to do is practice. You can unclip and clip in at any point while you're moving out on the road, or you can do it more safely on the turbo. If you have rollers, it's probably best not to ride them clipped in until you have thoroughly mastered the technique – or have something at hand to grab onto just in case. Practice, practice and practice and then, out on the road, make your decision early and unclip well before you come to a stop. It's far better to freewheel to a junction with a foot hanging, ready to put down, than to get there under full steam and run out of time and balance.

Don't be put off if you can't get the hang of clipping in and out as there's no rule that says you have to use clipless pedals. Get a good set of flat pedals (and, as is always the case with cycling, you can find shoes to match) and off you go! I always remember those pedals I had as a kid – metal with serrated edges for grip – which were highly adept at spinning round and taking a chunk out of your shin should you slip off one. I think there are probably much safer options on the market these days although, if you want to relive old times, I'm sure you could find a set. Flat pedals have the advantage that you can quickly and easily drop a foot to the ground, should the need occur.

I don't think it's coincidence that, in all my years riding around as a youngster, I rarely came off, and there were many occasions when I rode down a road or round a bend on two wheels and the sole of a trainer. My two recent accidents involving skids left me on the floor: had I been able to instinctively put a foot down at the time, I'm pretty certain I would have stayed upright or, at the very least, cushioned my fall. I can still vividly recall, on our ride back in 1984 (or '85), when Tommo clipped a kerb with his pedal and nearly lost it coming down the hill into Macclesfield. We must have been doing at least thirty miles per hour, and the only way he saved himself was by frantically hopping along until he got his bike back under control. Riding behind, I was laughing my head off but, looking back, it could have been so much different, especially had he been clipped into his pedals. (It was funny at the time, though.)

18. CRAMP

Cramp is not nice, especially if it hits you when you are out of the saddle, halfway up a steep climb. Leg muscles shoot with pain and you are virtually immobilised. Usually, once cramping has begun, it is not a one-off, and every time you have to do anything more than soft pedal, the spasms return. There are various theories as to why cramps visit us – ranging from lack of nutrition, or water, or electrolytes, to muscle fatigue, to bike set up – but nobody has yet found a definitive answer.

I used to get cramps on every sportive I did. The constant here was that I was riding hard for generally up to eighty miles (sometimes longer) but I would always feel the first spasms at about the forty-mile mark. I increased on-board food and I drank more, but to no avail, and the cramps kept hitting. Then, it suddenly occurred to me that, as well as being easier whatever the terrain, my usual Sunday rides were always about thirty-five miles long. Could it be that, even though I was plainly physically fit enough, my legs were simply not used to doing that extra distance and complaining when asked to do so?

Gradually, I increased my Sunday distances to the point now where, most Sundays, I'll ride around fifty to sixty miles. My legs are well used to spending up to four hours whizzing round and pressing down hard on the pedals. I haven't had cycling cramp in five years.

I'm not saying that this is the answer,* but it is something that has worked for me. I still make sure that I eat and drink enough.

[*This should be the subtitle to this book.]

July 11th 2016
5am
The forecast over the weekend said that there was going to be a change in the weather: the Mistral is on its way and it might well affect the Tour's Ventoux finish on Thursday 14th. It's a good job I've decided to make my own ascent today.

As it is, it looks like it might be a long, hot day, so I'm up to recheck all the things I checked last night. Then it's the usual breakfast of muesli, Greek yogurt and honey while I watch the pair of black redstarts in our little courtyard garden as they dart to and fro' from their cranny in the wall. Hopefully, we'll see the young before we leave. It's much more difficult to get the oats and nuts down today, even with extra honey. I'm thinking only one thing:

"Be careful, Ferdi! The Ventoux is a climb like no other!"*

I have had the phrase quietly running through my head for months, but it's now reaching a crescendo. (My name isn't even Ferdi, ffs!) The confidence that was streaming through me after Friday's ride up the Montagne de Lure is ebbing away and my excitement is tempered by nerves. I'm subdued – lost in my own little apprehensive world. Can I really do this?

Shelly can sense my nerves and so is equally quiet. I get dressed, which doesn't take long at all. Shorts, socks, shoes can wait 'til we get there, and jersey. I had brought my polka dot jersey with me, but wasn't going to wear it. Shelly pointed out last night that, if I couldn't wear it on a day like today, when could I wear it and I'd regret it if I didn't. I put it on, but with a pang of trepidation that it might bring me a bit of grief on a mountainside full of cycling fans camping out for the Tour stage in three days' time. Well, we'll see.

We pack the car – bike, track pump, water bottles, extra water, gels, pain au chocolat, and a change of clothes for when I'm finished – and then we're off. Savoillan is almost exactly opposite Bédoin across the mountain and so we could go clockwise or anticlockwise to get there. We decide the anticlockwise route via Malaucène.

It's just gone seven by the time we get to Bédoin, and the town's still waking up. Still intending to complete the Club des Cingles, I need to get my ticket stamped, so we stop by a café. The owner duly stamps away, but doesn't seem the happiest of chaps. Perhaps he was assuming we might stay for coffee and croissants. We pick up some more pain au chocolats from a boulangerie (you can never have enough), and then it's back to the car park for the off.

The sun is just starting to burn off what little early morning cloud there had been. It's going to be another beautiful day.

[*A mini Greek tragedy of a man beaten by his own hubris. If you don't know it, look it up!]

19. MECHANICAL!

Any sort of mechanical problem can really take the shine off a ride. Whether it be something as catastrophic as a broken wheel or rear mech hanger – which, try as you might, you will not be able to remedy with your multitool – to something as simple as a puncture. Chances are, you'll be stopped by the side of the road for a while, sometimes in the cold and rain, and will spend the rest of your ride with oil-stained hands. Chances also are, that riders will pass, ask "You alright?" to which, however bad things look, you'll reply, "Yep. All fine, cheers!" There's a guy in our Sunday group who, I think, I have yet to ride with where one problem or another has not beset him – sometimes, he hasn't even managed to reach the rendezvous. Fortunately, we have another member who seems to carry everything but a bike repair stand. Between us, we can usually get the unlucky one back on the road in one way or another, which is one benefit of riding in a group.

Sometimes, seemingly smaller issues can cause the biggest problems…
It was Good Friday and I had decided to do a lumpy, 55-mile loop around the Derbyshire-Yorkshire border. Parking in Glossop, to the east of Manchester, my ride was to take me over the Snake Pass, dropping down past the Ladybower Reservoir and towards Sheffield, before which I'd turn north onto The Strines, carry on over to

Holmfirth, then over Holme Moss and back down into Glossop.

It is very much one of those rides where you begin to doubt your own sanity in choosing the route when you're halfway around: there's a flat bit on a bridge over one arm of the reservoir, and that's about it. The Snake and Holme Moss are tough climbs on their own but The Strines, sitting in the middle, is the killer.

The Strines is actually Mortimer Road, which was named after an 18th Century chap called Mortimer, Lord of the Manor of nearby Bamford, who was instrumental in the passing of the act to get what had been little more than a dirt track repaired and widened. I have yet to find any of his rides on Strava. I assume that it takes its 'Strines' moniker from either or all of the Strines Inn, Strines Dyke and Reservoir that lie on its route, and it is a rollercoasting ten miles that runs, north–south, to join one Manchester to Sheffield road with another. When the Tour de France came (the following year, in fact, the Tour de France visited and took a route over Holme Moss and The Strines before finishing in Sheffield. They had the joy of newly surfaced roads. Ah, the joy!) they rode it from the north, which meant that they were straight into the climbing (it was given the moniker Côte de Midhopestones). From the south, the entry is more forgiving, but the short climbs are more savage, as the road dives into and out of deep valleys along the hillside, and the worst bit, Ewden Bank, is left 'til last. It's not dissimilar to doing a forty-minute HIIT session on the turbo. It really is a bit of a bugger.

I'd ridden it the previous year, also on a Good Friday. On that occasion, a half day in the fishmonger's had meant I'd had a free afternoon. All my gear was packed into the van in the morning and everything was going to plan as I shut the door at one o'clock, the only fly in the ointment being that, in my haste to get out of the shop and on my ride, I had cut myself quite badly on one of the knives whilst washing up. I found a number of plasters and bound my finger and it seemed to have stopped bleeding by the time I arrived in Glossop but, after a few miles of riding, my hand began to leak again. I suppose my body position was quite far away from the recommended "hold the injury higher up than your heart", but what was I supposed to do? Go home?

By the time I had made my way onto The Strines, my front forks and right leg were covered in blood. It just would not stop bleeding. Halfway along, I had the good fortune to find an old couple sat by the side of the road, enjoying the Easter sunshine and just about to tuck into their picnic. I pulled over and asked if they had any kitchen towel. The lady blanched as she stared at my crimson-stained body and bike. Fortunately, they managed to quickly find me a couple of paper napkins and asked what manner of awful cycling accident had led to my injury.

"Oh no," I replied cheerily, "I did this before I came!"

I wound the napkins tightly around my finger and left them, I like to think, ever-so-slightly bemused. Luckily, the paper did the job at stemming the blood, but holding onto it made gripping the bars a little tricky, especially on the fast descent off Holme Moss. Fast descents can be great fun if you have a smooth road and two good hands: unfortunately, I had neither, and I dropped off that hill so carefully that I almost needed new brake blocks by the time I got to the bottom. The blood had now dried, but I continued to get some quizzical looks from eagle-eyed onlookers until I arrived back at the van in Glossop.

Back to a year later, and I was once more on The Strines on Good Friday, with just the toughest bit, Ewden Bank, to go, and I heard the dreaded hiss of the puncture. It was the rear wheel, as usual. I didn't have a repair kit on me, but had brought a couple of spare tubes, so I sat on the side of the road for five minutes, changed over, and I was on my way again. I struggled up Ewden Bank (1km, average gradient 12%, maxing at around 18% a couple of times) and was halfway into the drop to the main road when the wheel started hissing again. Cursing my luck, I pulled over, took the inner tube out and checked the tyre for thorns, but there was nothing to feel, so I put my second tube in inflated it, and set off again. Three hundred yards down the road, the rear wheel deflated again.

I was not a happy bunny. I did not have a puncture repair kit with me (two spare tubes are normally more than enough) but I was not unduly worried as I thought I could probably cadge another tube from the next passing rider.

I sat on the wall to wait.

And I waited.

And waited.

Half an hour passed and still nobody came by! Outside a house at the bottom of the road I saw two men talking, so I click-clacked down to them and asked if they could help. Neither had a repair kit, but one said he was just about to go and see his girlfriend in Leeds and he would be passing a Halford's, which he reckoned would still be open on Good Friday and was "only five minutes down the road". This was marvellous news, so I put the bike in the back of his van, and off we went.

Twelve miles later, we arrived at the Halford's. (I sensed we were going further than I'd originally assumed when we crossed the M1 motorway and started seeing signs that said, "Barnsley 1 mile".) The further we got, the more I began to worry that (a) my driver did not have a girlfriend in Leeds but a shack in the woods and (b) it was going to be one hell of a tough ride back into a headwind. Eventually, we pulled into the Halford's store and I spent the money I had with me on three new tubes, installed one in the shop so I could avail myself of their track pump, and returned to the van where, thankfully, the chap had decided that he'd return me from whence we came.

Halfway back, there was a loud bang. We looked at each other and then I reached behind to check the bike - my new innertube had just exploded. My chauffeur was sympathetic, but he could do no more than he already had, and left me back on the roadside at the foot of the Côte de Midhopestones.

I sat on the verge and set about looking for the reason for my predicament and, eventually, discovered that I had a small tear in the wall of the tyre. (Still, no cyclists went by – did they know something I did not??) I found that the brake block on one side had been installed ever-so-slightly too high so that it had been rubbing on the tyre every time I pulled the lever, and it had decided that this was the best time and place to finally wear it through. I was down to two tubes and still had twenty miles to go to get back to my van, most of it downhill. There would be much braking ahead, but I knew from my return from Barnsley that I wouldn't need to brake to cause a blow-out. What was I to do?

I knocked on the door of the house where the other man lived, which was answered by his wife. After a few minutes' searching, she came out with a resigned look on her face and a roll of picture framing tape, apologising that this was all she had. I covered the inside of the tyre in the stuff, put the tube in, and gingerly pumped it up again. I waited ten minutes – amazingly, it held. I rode up and down the road a few times – it still held. Now all I had to do was ride home into a stiff headwind as gently as possible. Needless to say, I did not break any records, and could almost have got off and walked on the final descent into Glossop, which took me over a number of speed bumps, but I did make it back to the van without having to stop again*.

The Theory of Cycling Relativity: Law 20
Punctures can last much longer than you anticipate after you've fixed them.

This refers to what I term 'puncture scar'. You go out on a ride, and you get a puncture (usually on the back wheel – it's always the bloody back wheel), and you fix it, either by repairing, or simply chucking on a fresh tube. You spend a considerable amount of sweat and bicep inflating it with that little pump, and then you ride on.

But the puncture isn't finished with you because, for the rest of that ride, and possibly well into the next ride you do, you are absolutely convinced that you still have a puncture. You spend your whole time staring at the point where your tyre meets the road, trying to discern if it's flat or not. Has it always squished out like that? Can you feel more tarmac than you normally would? This is the psychological scar that a puncture can leave, and it can ruin a ride. It can play havoc with your mind and, consequently, I have ridden on with a real puncture so convinced was I that I was just imagining it.

[*Sometimes, this world can be a crappy place, but the kindness of strangers never ceases to amaze me.]

20. TO SHAVE OR NOT TO SHAVE

It's a thing, isn't it, male cyclists shaving their legs? For years, I didn't – now, I do.
Why?

There are many reasons flying around as to why many male cyclists* shave their legs, such as the fact that it's more aerodynamic and so makes you faster, or that it helps if you need to attend to road rash or cuts and grazes. Certainly, there might be a case for the latter. Cleaning a wound, especially if you are particularly hairy, will be easier and, more importantly – and I have had painful experience of this – changing dressings on hairless skin is far more desirable. Oddly, we don't feel the need to also shave our arms and, at the present time, there are a fair few (and not inconsiderable) beards in the pro peloton, but it does appear that there is a quantifiable power saving to be made by shaving your legs. As with all things to do with cycling power, the faster you want to go, the more power you have to put in, and so the greater saving will be made. If you're comfortable zipping about at 25-30mph and after shaving seconds off your ten-mile time trial, then you should get the razor out, but if you're used to pootling around at under 10mph, I would not expect to get much benefit from newly shaved limbs.

Why did I decide to shave? Well, the primary and original reason was because I was finding it difficult/annoying spreading sun cream over my reasonably hairy limbs for summer rides. Lotion, especially if it was thicker, was just getting stuck in the hairs and I could never be certain of an even coverage before I went out. The second reason, which is a consequence of the first, is that it just looks better. I now have a seamless, smooth line all the way down, through shorts, thighs, shins to socks where, before, it was all fuzzy in the middle.

TAKING THE PLUNGE
The initial shave can be a psychologically difficult moment. It's a little like bungee jumping – once you've started, there's no going back (although, there is a point in bungee jumping where you do go back, otherwise something has gone terribly, terribly wrong). It's also likely to create a bit of a mess in the sink/shower/bath, particularly for the more hirsute amongst you. Therefore, I would recommend, before getting the razor out, doing the first cut outside with a set of clippers. Then, once you have removed the longer hairs, you can apply your foam of choice and carefully begin the shave. It's always tricky to get the bits at the back of the knee and, since it's not anything like a flat surface there, there is a risk of the odd nick, so be extra cautious.

Of course, down the bottom end, it's easy to decide where to stop, but where do you end the shave up at the top (which is, oddly, also the bottom end)? You should go higher than your cycling shorts hem because you have to think that, at some point the chances are you will be wearing shorts that are shorter: football shorts, tennis or squash shorts, or even swimming trunks. If you believe having shaved legs looks a bit odd, think about the image you'll be projecting if hair suddenly starts growing north of a line just above your knees. The best course of action is to shave up as far as you dare. The hair is thinner up here anyway, and so it takes less work - but don't forget to do the corresponding height at the back, too.

Once you have completed your task, you will notice three things. Firstly, those aren't your legs that you're looking down at. I'll always remember the day that I decided, because my bald spot had become so obvious, to go off and have my head shaved. The oddest thing was not the guy looking back from the mirror (which was, of course, different...but still rather handsome), or the feeling, when I walked out of the barber's, of breeze against my scalp: it was seeing my shadow on the ground which was now that of a person with a round head and sticky out ears. I knew that this was my shadow but...this was not my shadow! It's exactly the same with your legs: you know that they're yours – they're stuck to your hips for a start – but the view you've had for years and years is totally different.

Secondly, it does all feel a bit weird, especially if you immediately put on a pair of trousers. There is no longer that layer to come between skin and material and so the touch you feel is very different to what you've been used to for most of your life. In my experience, it takes a couple of days to fully acclimatise.

The third thing is that, even if you have done a great job, just like cleaning your bike it's most likely that you'll find a bit that you've missed. With me, it's somewhere around the kneecaps and I usually find it while I'm sat on the loo and so not far from the razor to remedy the oversight. It is often a "how the hell did I miss that???" moment but it's my belief that the hairs you miss only come out from hiding when they think it's safe a couple of hours later, so always be prepared for stragglers.

(There is a fourth thing which is, if you have legs like mine, jealousy from your spouse/partner. This extends to envy and admiration up and down our road. I am at pains to point out to Shelly that much hard work has gone into the making of my legs and that she too could have pins almost as great, if only she put the effort in. This is not, apparently, what she is wanting to hear.)

So, now that you have stripped your legs bare you are faced with the additional upkeep. It pays to keep on top of the situation as those hairs will start to grow back and stubble is the in-between stage that nobody wants. You could leave every shave to the morning of a ride – who cares if nobody is going to see those legs, eh? – but it is far easier to shave often so that your legs remain bare and smooth. This way, if you miss some hair one day, you're more than likely to find it the next. And, much like a lawn, the longer you leave it, the bigger the job to mow.

It is for this reason that, this year, I continued shaving right the way through the winter. It had, up until now, been a personal tradition to cease shearing when the weather became cold enough to necessitate leg warmers or tights. There was no point with the upkeep, I thought, if they were not to be on show. Then, every spring, usually when the clocks went forward to BST at the end of March, I would have the Grand Unveiling and attend to what had lain fallow over the previous few months. The problem here was that every year, because all the hair had regrown, I was taken back to the beginning and that giant initial shave. Much as it was a physical and psychological ceremony that heralded the warmer weather, I decided that it was one I could well do without and it was much simpler (like the lawn) to keep mowing through the winter so that the first cut of spring was not such a mammoth task.

Now I have beautiful legs all year round!

[*Obviously, female cyclists shave their legs too, but this seems to be part of day-to-day feminine upkeep, as opposed to specifically for cycling, and so they come to the sport with pre-shaved legs. If you're a female who does not normally shave their legs, but has done just to ride a bike, I apologise for the generalisation.]

21. HOW TO AVOID SQUIRRELS

If you haven't done much riding, you might not be aware of the danger they pose to cyclists and themselves but, much like pedestrians, squirrels occasionally get the urge to run across the road in front of you when you're least expecting it. The difference between the two is that the former do not generally tend to have fluffy tails and the latter have an inbuilt escape mechanism that might be perfect for evading hawks or dogs but gives the cyclist a problem.

The difficulty arises because a squirrel, in moments of danger, does not run in straight lines, and will usually dart back on itself at least a couple of times in order to confuse its attacker before leaving the immediate vicinity at top speed. The cyclist will spot the rodent venturing across a road or trail and will naturally veer slightly to carry on behind it, but the squirrel will then employ its tactic and end up back in the path of the oncoming wheels. The cyclist veers the other way only to find that our furry friend has done a one-eighty and is still there. All of this happens within a second or less, depending upon the speed of the bike.

You could just slam on the brakes but, if you're zipping along at high speed and the road is anything other than bone dry, you're risking a skid and possible fall.

What to do, then?

Well, you cannot second-guess a squirrel. Half the time, they don't even know what they're doing. The best thing is to carry straight on, and you'll find that instincts will usually direct the squirrel away. I say "usually"... Once, I saw a squirrel remarkably run between two bikes (and four wheels!) that were bombing along at top speed in front of me. It lost part of its tail, but made it through. More recently, I employed my 'straight ahead' strategy only to find that the squirrel had had the same idea. Odd feeling, that, running over a squirrel with your rear wheel. (I stopped, but it had still managed to dive into a hedge and away.)

22. HOW TO AVOID MOTORISTS

Dangerous as squirrels might be, they are no match for motor vehicles. It is one of life's tragedies that one of the most enjoyable things you can do for a fit mind and body carries the caveat that, one day, you might not come home. One should not let this fact ruin a ride: you can't spend all your time worrying that, somewhere, there's a car, lorry or bus with your name on it. While, in the UK over the past few years, cyclists and motorists may not be at the point of all out war that elements of the media would have us believe, it is true that, from time to time, we do not share the road as well as we might. Much of this comes down to attitude. I, myself, know that I have a completely different attitude when I'm behind the wheel of a car.

**The Theory of Cycling Relativity:
Law 21
Most cyclists are motorists, too.
(A fact often missed by non-cycling motorists, especially when baying for cyclists to pay 'road tax', which is not actually a thing and is itself a fact rarely missed by cyclists.)**

Behind the wheel of a car, I am far more impatient and irritable. Most of the other motorists are, by turns, idiots and arseholes, who should not be in charge of anything more basic than a shopping trolley. Oddly, whatever my mood, I am highly deferential towards cyclists and horse riders – especially if the latter is aboard a horse – and give both a wide berth. Pedestrians are fine, so long as they're on the pavement but, when they do that crossing-the-road-without-looking thing, I get very annoyed. Driving requires enough concentration already without having to worry about people throwing themselves in front of you. And runners/joggers! Why do you have to run on the road when there's a perfectly good footpath available?? It's no wonder some cyclists use the pavement – it's to avoid all the runners!

I believe the motorist's attitude towards the cyclist can be summed up in this little vignette:

There is a stretch of road nearby, between my house and a roundabout, which is roughly a mile long and difficult to undertake a safe overtake. One day, whilst in the car, I was caught in a queue behind a tractor as it trundled, at about twenty mph, along, on its way to some field or other. I was ten cars back in a line of perhaps twenty. It was a hot day, everyone had their windows down, and you could hear a mixture of different songs from different radios. We all processed slowly to the roundabout, where, thankfully, the tractor turned off one way and most of the cars turned the other. It was the very essence of patience.

A week later, I rode that same stretch on my bike and, due to the relative flatness of gradient, was able to hold a constant speed that was almost tractor-like in its twenty mphness. Behind me, I had grown a tail of cars. Highly aware that they would want to pass, I rode as close to the potholes and hedges as I safely could, although I knew I was well within my rights (and would be in far less danger) if I held the centre of the lane. Rather than sit patiently behind me, as they had with the tractor. The motorists beeped their horns and revved their engines, and the car immediately behind me spent the time jumping forward to almost touch my rear wheel and then falling back slightly. When, eventually – it actually was a matter of around three minutes – we reached the roundabout, the cars were free to go past. It was a hot day, everyone had their windows down, and I heard a mixture of different curses from different drivers.

The motorcade queue formed by a cyclist or cyclists can be similarly angry when riding up a long climb, particularly if it's a twisty, turny thing. As I am a motorist in my other life, I am well aware of the anguish I am causing, but there are times when there's no bloody way I'm going to pull over and stop to let cars go by. I did it on the Bealach-Na-Ba in Scotland and the gradient (15%) and narrowness (very) of the road was such that I couldn't clip in and set off again. I actually had to flag down a car that was descending towards me so that I could hold onto its side to get going. Thankfully, the occupants were cycling-friendly Dutch – they even offered to give me a lift to the top! I see it that, as the physical pain has to be endured by the cyclist when journeying up a climb, so the motorist has a massive test of patience.

The irony is, of course, that you let the car pass only to be held up by it going down the other side, and there is little chance of the driver letting you go by to continue your journey. This is always something you should bear in mind, especially when, if you do let the car by, you are often thanked with insults. It's a funny thing, though, because, most of the time, although you get the gist, you seldom hear what is actually said by disgruntled drivers. This is because of the law of sonic physics which is:

The Theory of Cycling Relativity:
Law 22
Cars cocoon pithy comments.

So far, I've only had rural cycling in mind. Urban cycling can be a much more intense experience. I'd say, "Don't do that urban cycling, dude!", but you're quite likely to commute by bike, so you don't really have much choice. All would be fine if everyone commuted by bike but this, quite plainly, is not the case and so cyclists and motorists are squeezed into confined spaces at the most hectic times. Attitudes are intensified – on both sides – and all see flagrant disregard of the rules of the road.

The Theory of Cycling Relativity: Law 23
If we can successfully avoid cars, we will quite likely outlive their occupants. (I believe that motorists know this and that their antipathy is fuelled, in part, by jealousy.)

Motorists seldom keep to speed limits, constantly drive far too close to the car in front, park illegally (but that's just fine because they've put their hazard lights on), fail to signal when turning or changing lanes, use their phones whilst driving (not only to talk but to text!!!), and even read and eat whilst driving. (I once drew alongside a car and heard that the occupant was having a phone conversation on her hands-free system – which was just fine – because she needed her hand to hold the spoon to eat the bowl of cereal that was sitting in her lap – which was not fine. I then watched her pull away to join the motorway.) They then see the odd cyclist jumping a red light and become understandably infuriated. Weaving in and out of traffic, cyclists can become an unwanted distraction, just another thing for drivers to worry about (or not, as the case may be), but isn't everything on an urban road something to worry about?

A few years ago, to avoid points on my licence, I attended a Speed Awareness Course. At one point, we were asked to watch a short film of a car driving down an urban street and note the potential hazards. The piece lasted perhaps a couple of minutes. We watched, we noted, and, at the end, we totted up our hazards. In a room of around thirty motorists, results ranged between two and twelve. I had thirty-five. Turned out I was the only cyclist. When asked why my number was so high, I replied that I see everything as a potential hazard.*

[*As we all left the car park at the end of the day, I have never seen the speed limit broken so much, by so many people, at the same time. I guess the course had a lasting effect.]

This is something I don't think non-cyclists ever consider. We may look like we are taking huge risks and zipping along without a care in the world, but we are actually simply more attuned to the road. We do not sit in metal boxes, most are not listening to music or talking to others on the phone, we are higher up and so have a higher and wider field of view than most motorists, and, if we are not already greatly aware of our own vulnerability on the road, we are constantly reminded of it. Life-long cyclists are far better equipped and attuned to the road and its conditions and far less likely to take risks than motorists do.

The safest way to ride is to hold the middle of a lane, but you know that you will then be holding up the traffic, so you tend drift to the side. This allows any motorists to get past but leaves you open to the dangers of The Two Ps – potholes and pedestrians. The former lurk below, looking to give you anything from a pinch puncture to a broken bone, the latter like to leap out without a moment's notice. Add to this ever-present risks such as grids and the opening car door, and there are dangers everywhere.

The Theory of Cycling Relativity: Law 24
The vehicle that is least able to cope with the worst bits of road is the one that is most often forced to ride there.

Taking a place towards the middle of the lane keeps you further away from these risks and, importantly, it will block traffic behind and prevent them having to make stupid decisions, such as "I can probably just squeeze past that cyclist as we go between these bollards" or "I should be able to make it to that left-hand turn first". It's impatience, mixed with bad decisions or plain old indecision, that is the enemy. There are choices that might end with damage to vehicular paintwork for them, much worse for you. If there's a choice to be made between getting called a wanker or ending up in casualty, it's not much of a choice.

There are times when you must claim the centre of a lane – if you're turning, is one – but, if you're out and about on faster, wider, rural roads, it seems to be a given that you keep to one side to let motor traffic flow by. Still, given all the room in the world, many drivers seem oblivious to the danger they present to cyclists and, rather than overtake on the other side of the road, as they would if they were going around a slower car, they give cyclists a close pass.

Close passing can be hugely stressful. I have had probably five occasions that I would term 'near death'. Twice, a lorry has been so close going by that its wing mirror passed directly over my head, only just missing me. (The incidents were about twenty years apart, so I don't think it was the same lorry.) In between, I was nearly flattened by a driver in their impatience to get by a slow-moving gravel wagon coming up a hill I was descending. Luckily, I had had a good long view of the traffic train snaking its way towards me and suspected something like this might happen. I was ready to take avoiding action, but it was still a shock that, even when we passed within inches of each other, the driver did not appear to notice me.

More recently, I have nearly met my maker whilst dropping down hills on reasonably steep single-track roads. The first time, a lorry driver inexplicably decided that it would be better for him not to turn into the layby on his side of the road, forcing me to slam on the brakes and divert my approach towards the twelve-inch gap he'd left me. Fortunately, I am quite narrow, and so just made it. More hair-raising than that was rounding a bend on a similarly narrow descent to come face to face with a fork-lift truck carrying scaffolding at exactly head height. This time, there was nowhere to go as the metal pipes perfectly fitted the width of the road. I managed to hold a straight skid on a dry and dusty surface and came to rest with inches to spare.

"That could've really put a dampener on the weekend!" I said cheerily to the ashen-faced driver. I have rarely been so relieved. The rest of that ride, I'm sure the sun shone a little brighter.

I have also been forced into the verge and off my bike by a car trying to squeeze past up a narrow hill road. Not to mention the countless times I have nearly been taken out by cars pulling out of side roads. And I count myself lucky. (I hope Shelly doesn't read this bit!) I spend much time baffled at the lack of awareness of motorists but there are still many times that I'll get a close pass that will be almost inexplicable. Usually, it occurs when a stream of cars has the chance to overtake. Car one, two and three will give me due consideration and a wide berth but then, for some reason, car four will nearly take my elbow off. What has car four been looking at while the cars in front have been manoeuvring around me? Why have they not thought "Oh, that's a good idea!" and followed suit? Did I bully them in school? Have they been reading my Twitter feed? Are they transfixed by my perfectly honed backside? (It can happen.)

One motorists' bugbear is that cyclists persist in riding two abreast on country roads. Given that the drivers should afford us the same courtesy as another car and cross to the other side of the road when overtaking, we could legitimately ride three or four abreast, as long as we do not spill over into that other lane. It is a much longer manoeuvre to overtake ten riders in single file than ten riding two abreast. By riding next to each other, we are doing motorists a favour. When they yell their muffled, unintelligible curses at you on the way past, be sure to point that out.

They do say that, before you judge a person, you should walk a mile in their shoes (let's hope they don't have tiny feet). Similarly, it might be good if motorists, as part of their driving test, were asked to take on a bike for a week and ride it around, just to see the view from the gutter. From her limited experience on two wheels, Shelly readily admits that she now has a completely different outlook and is far more patient* and watchful when encountering cyclists on the road. This is certainly not an exercise in motorist bashing and when drivers are up in arms (which is a dangerous thing to do whilst in charge of a heavy vehicle) over large groups of riders mobbing the road, I think that maybe they have a point.

Opinions have become so polarised that both sides go onto the roads expecting a battle: I've seen riders demonstrating a bloody-minded attitude and holding the middle of the road when it would have been be far easier for all concerned to pull in and let a few cars go past. That sense of victory they might have had must have been tinged with so much stress over the situation that it cannot have been worth the effort. Much as you feel that they are out to get you, we all share the same space, so be nice.

[*This is not something I have noticed at home.]

23. ETIQUETTE

Etiquette
noun
"the customary code of polite behaviour in society or among members of a particular profession or group."

Over the years, road cyclists have developed a system of signals that help them get along with both each other and the condition of the roads themselves. It's a series of shouts and arm gestures to communicate and to alert others of potential danger. It works very well on group rides, where hazards can be quickly pointed out to a rider behind who may not be able to fully see what is coming up in front.

As with any form of language, a failure to properly comprehend can sometimes result in unintended offence. During my first sportive, I sat for some miles behind another rider, hiding in his slipstream to benefit from the much easier ride. A number of times I saw his right elbow jerk outward, each time getting more pronounced. At the time, I thought he had something wrong with him: now, I know that he wanted me to come past and do my fair share. As it was, he was slowly getting ever more frustrated as I remained happy to be sat in his wake, transfixed on his arm and trying to guess when next it would move: if only he'd have said something! At that time, I was mostly riding solo, or with fellow neophytes, so there was nobody to teach me these things and it was only when I saw the pros on the tv doing the same thing that I worked out what it meant. Boy, he must have been getting mad (but, given my condition in that first sportive, he was probably much better off with me behind).

Karma is a thing, obviously, and the same has happened to me while out on a ride. On the way back from a particularly hilly jaunt to the Peak District (the clue, as ever, is in the name) I overtook two riders before turning off onto a more minor road. I was aware, as I turned, that at least one of the pair had followed me but paid it no mind. This five-mile stretch of road was slightly downhill over its length, but undulating and, this day, into a headwind. I put my hands on to the drops, got my head down and pedalled hard. Still, I could sense I was not alone but, since I was not racing and merely wanting to get home for some scrambled eggs and avocado on bagels (the usual post-ride fare), I wasn't bothered in the slightest. Occasionally, the sun would come out and my passenger's shadow would betray him. I thought it odd since, if roles were reversed and I was able to be close enough to another rider to actually pass them, I would, and quickly too – otherwise you get that slightly awkward moment when you're there too many seconds past your "Morning!". I continued and we neared the end of the stretch, where the road first dips, and then bends up quickly over a humpbacked railway bridge. As we rounded the bend and started the rise, I got out of the saddle to ride up the lump to find myself being overtaken. My erstwhile trailer launched past me

in a full-on Mark Cavendish sprint, crested the top of the bridge and celebrated with a fist pump and a quiet, but still audible "Yes!"
I don't know what he'd won – although I suspect it has much to do with the word 'segment' – but he never thanked me. It was all most bizarre. (Had he not then gone straight on at the crossroads where I was turning left, I would have been severely tempted to follow him up to the next railway bridge and win that pretend sprint.)

More seasoned as I am now, and well used to riding in groups, it has become second nature to automatically point at all sorts of stuff. Usually, and not surprisingly when riding on British roads, it's potholes and grids*, then parked cars (signalled by an arm across the back, pointing away from the hazard). Gravel or hugely uneven surfaces are signalled by a wavy hand. Because it's a given that signals will be used, when somebody neglects to use one, and you're the one confidently riding behind who ends up in the hole, it's bloody annoying.
[*Ever noticed that, when they actually do get around to repairing a stretch of road, the chaps involved very rarely raise a grid in line with the new level of surfacing? As a result, the ironwork gradually gets deeper and deeper. There are grids near me that could more accurately be described as wells.]

Vocal signals seem to vary geographically. Where we ride, an oncoming car is "Car up!" and one arriving from behind is "Car back!". "HOLE!"

is rarely used, but comes if a rider is physically unable or just not quick enough to point out a pothole below.

And, of course, no matter how I am feeling, whether I'm flying along a flat or grovelling up a 20% incline, I will always give a cheery "Morning!/Afternoon!/Evening!" as I pass another rider on the road. Those coming the other way, well, at the very least, they receive The Wave.

THE CYCLIST'S WAVE
Ah, The Wave. The Cyclist's Wave. That sign of recognition from one knight of the road to another. This is never an overt gesture, it's something altogether more subtle: a brief palm point, often without taking one's hand off the bars; sometimes just a single finger (but not the same one we use for motorists); and sometimes, get this, it's not a wave at all, but a nod of the head. However it might be communicated, however fleeting, it is an important sign that pays respect to a fellow two-wheeled user of the highway.

This being the case, when a wave is not returned, when a nod is ignored, when the rider just passes you without even a flicker that they have noticed you, then this is a slight that can ruin a ride and have you muttering to yourself for miles and miles. How bloody dare they not wave! Do they think they are too good to let on??? It's the equivalent of ignoring someone who holds a door open for you or failing to acknowledge the other driver who patiently waits to let you go through that bottleneck first. IT'S JUST NOT ON!

This is an insult that can be magnified exponentially if you come across a whole group of riders who glide by without any sort of response to your goodwill gesture. There is a club local to me who consistently fail to raise a single finger between the lot of them. On the first few occasions, I found this quite maddening, but I came to the conclusion that, rather than get upset about it, I would turn it into a bit of fun. Now, if I meet them on the road, they are greeted with a wild Forrest Gump/Lieutenant Dan-type wave, accompanied by an individual "Morning!/Afternoon!/Evening!" for each of them. I'm not certain how they take it, but it cheers me up no end.

Etiquette towards everyone else on the road should be a given. It costs nothing to be polite. I've spoken about motorists in the previous section and, yes, sometimes it's tough not to react, but it is nice when we all get along (or you can, if you prefer, just be smug that you were the bigger person).

And it's not just motor traffic. Always slow and give as much room to horses as you can. When I'm approaching from the back, I like to call, "Coming up behind", which lets the rider know I am there and has the added bonus that it has just a hint of the double entendre. It's the same with pedestrians who, especially out in the countryside on summer days, you can often find in family groups, strewn right across the road. It's as though all the trees, hedges, birdsong and the absence of pavement bewilders them into a feeling of utter safety.

Perhaps, like a group of meerkats, they think that at least one of them will be keeping watch, but it's not uncommon to be able to get right up to them without being noticed. A cheery "Morning!/Afternoon/Evening!" when you get about twenty yards away usually does a good trick of dispersing them. This also doubles up as a greeting: I acknowledge everyone I meet on a ride. Even if I'm not on the bike and we're out walking the dogs, I will say my "hellos", and I do get a little annoyed if we are ridden by and ignored by steely-faced cyclists, just because we are not, apparently, part of their tribe. Shelly says that they don't know I'm also a cyclist when I'm out and about disguised as a walker, but that's not the point. It's simply good manners, and any happy interaction will brighten the day.

BELLS

I'm not a fan of the bicycle bell. It lies somewhere between littering and people who stand still in the middle of an escalator in my "Things I Hate" list. I know it's seen as an ideal way to alert others as to your approach, but I find it massively impersonal. No! you say, it's a cheerful, happy sound! I don't think so. Often, especially on canal tow paths or, even worse, footpaths (the clue's in the name, dummy!), we will be walking along with the dogs and suddenly, from behind, we will get:

Ding-ding.

In what way is that more cheerful than a polite "Excuse me"?

Ding-ding.

Much like the car horn, there is no nuance to a bicycle bell and no matter how you intend to use it, it always comes out the same way:

Ding-ding – get out of the way.

Actually, you can vary a car horn's meaning, from a "Hello, Mrs Thornton!" toot-toot, to a full-on "WTF ARE YOU DOING!!!" blare.

This is something that a bell will not give you:

Ding-ding.

Or, if you are to be more insistent:

Ding-ding, ding-ding.

Horns work because the distances involved are generally further and the speeds at which people are likely to meet are faster. And drivers are inside a metal box, so shouting (as explained by TToCR: Law 22) is often ineffective. For we cyclists, there is usually ample time to call out and get the message across, if need be, without the need for a ding-ding.

I'm in a bad mood now.

24. PARTNERS

It might come as no surprise that Shelly suggested this as a subject for a chapter. It's highly probable that the vast majority of those reading this will have significant others and, of those, it is as likely that those partners will not view cycling as you do. Obviously, there will be the few couples who share the passion but, for many, cycling can be the third wheel in the relationship.

Shelly has come to understand just what a big part cycling plays in my life. Sometimes she becomes exasperated at the amount of my waking time it takes up (bizarrely, I have yet to have a cycling-specific dream) and, as I noted right at the beginning of the book, she has a very valid point. I do it, I watch it, I read about it, tweet about it and write about it. When I should be thinking about what colour to repaint the bedroom, I'm deciding whether to drop my bars a smidgen. I may look totally engaged in the viewing of emulsion colour cards, but my mind is actually on whether I have the right tools in the garage to cut down my own steerer tube or just take it in to my local bike shop and get them to do it for me.

I am in no denial. For my part, I try to keep off YouTube as much as I can while there is nothing live to watch on telly, and make a concerted effort to have every third book I read non-cycling. Added to this, I try to keep all my velothoughts to myself, although Shelly did once overhear me say "bottom bracket" out loud whilst smirking to myself.

She will not believe me, but every weekend ride I go on is planned with her wishes in mind so that I will be back in time to spend the majority of the rest of the day with her. Obviously, it's difficult on group rides to keep to a tight schedule, something which does play on my mind and can affect the enjoyment, especially if we are very late in returning. I'll spend the later miles and, if need be, drive home, thinking "Oo, she's not going to be happy."

For her part, Shelly does get involved. She likes to go out on the odd ride herself (as yet, it has to be not too far, no hills, sunny, still, warm), and feels good when we return, but doesn't ride often enough to raise her level. She now enjoys watching the cycling on tv. This was an interest initially piqued by the glorious scenery the Tour de France offers, but now she is reasonably au fait with tactics and terminology and, while she could not sit still in front of the screen for five hours, she likes to watch the mountain stages and is usually eager to see the finish. We've been together to see multiple stages of the Tour de France and Tour of Britain, and she is happy to ferry me over to Bakewell for the Tour of The Peak sportive, which is practically the same thing.

The main thing is that, although Shelly perhaps* feels that cycling takes up far too much space in my brain, she can see how happy it makes me and, I suppose, that makes her happy. She realises that this is something that keeps me not

just physically fit, but mentally fit. I am happy when I can ride. I spent around five or six years during my cycling hiatus playing golf: similarly, I might have been out for up to five hours, but I would always come home bloody frustrated, having hit as many roads, schools, pubs and clubhouses as I had greens. (I like to think that I played the game with a certain 'panache'. Fortunately, nobody ever got hurt.) Riding a bike, I never walk in the door in anything other than a good mood. Even on those occasions I broke my collarbone and wrist, I was cheerful.
[*definitely]

I might joke about it, but I'm grateful to the amount of leeway she gives me in pursuing my pastime. It was actually she who convinced me to buy my new bike, with me dithering over the question of "Yes, of course I want it, but do I really need it?" Our brains are set up very differently and, whereas "want" and "need" occupy pretty much the same space in her head, they are very far apart in mine. This, apparently, makes me a nightmare to buy presents for because I hate surprises - Shelly loves the look of awe on a face as a present is unwrapped, but buying for me is a risky business as I cannot hide my disappointment at an unwanted gift - and, come birthday or Christmas time, my usual answer to her "What do you want?" is "Well, I don't actually need anything". I'd genuinely rather have nothing than something I don't want. Partly, this is because I see it as a waste of money, but it is also because I know that Shelly will be deeply upset at my adverse reaction and so I'd rather avoid all that bother. Whatever I have needed throughout the year I have just bought as and when that need arose. I think this makes life simple and, when I say "Don't get me anything" I absolutely mean it. It is very different to her "Don't get me anything" which, if followed to the letter, would have my bags packed and on the doorstep. I didn't need a new bike – the one I had was perfectly good – and so I could happily have parked that feeling of want, but Shelly convinced me otherwise. And I bloody love my new bike, so she was right on that one.

She indulged me so far with our trips to Scotland and Provence just so I could ride up mountains there. She never fails to wish me a good ride when I leave the house and, as pissed off as she might be when I arrive back a little on the tardy side, she always wants to know where I/we have been on our travels.

And, there's always the fact, for her, living with a cyclist brings with it that constant element of anxiety when I go out which stays with her until I have returned, and returned in one piece. She worries far more about me cycling on our roads than I do, probably because she has seen, at close hand, the amount of accidents I have had around the house. It has been mentioned more than once that I should wear my helmet at all times.

Shelly is more than happy for me to keep the bikes inside the house, although she still thinks it's a little odd that I have to pat the saddle lovingly every time I pass the one in the kitchen.

Having said that, she was a bit put out that I got rid of the bed in the spare bedroom to afford my turbo trainer set-up the space I felt it deserved. (Her question, "But where will any guests stay?" was met with a happy, "Not here.")

It's not just cycling, cycling, cycling for me. We have always had dogs, and they play a massive part in our lives. They even get to go on holidays the bikes don't! As we aren't happy kennelling them, most of the holidays we have taken over the past twenty years have been based around the UK with the dogs and the bikes are left at home. (The Bealach-Na-Ba trip was very much an exception, with dogs and bikes filling the car. (God knows how we'd have gone on if we'd had children, too: they'd've been walking, I suppose.) When we did leave the dogs, to spend our fortnight in Provence, Shelly was in tears before we got to the end of the road. As I said, they're a BIG part of our lives.) We have been to some wonderful parts of the UK with them, and had fantastic, bike-free times. We do a lot of walking. Shelly knows me only too well, though, and has often looked over at me whilst I was driving through the countryside, noticed my wistful look and said, "You're thinking about what it would be like to ride your bike on this road, aren't you?" And it's true. So much so, that, on topsy-turvy, winding mountain roads, every gear change in the car would be coloured by what I would do on the bike. I'd even lean into corners. We have an automatic now, so it's not quite the same (but I still lean).

Some years ago, I bought Shelly a bike – a hybrid mountain/roadie thing – and some kit so she could come and join me, and hopefully catch the bug. It never quite turned out as I expected, and her rides are generally few and far between. Now, when I do get Shelly out, it's normally as part of my warm-down ride. I'll go out for my three, four or five hours and then, when I return, she will join me for a short, easy route around the local lanes – as long as it's warm and sunny. She remains ever concerned that, on these rides, she is slowing me down and curtailing my enjoyment but, for me, riding slowly is the whole point. If she weren't acting as my anchor (in the nicest, most positive sense of the word), I would speed round the circuit and totally defeat the object. Either that or just not do the extra spin at all. I want to ride slowly, and I love these little rides, as it allows Shelly to see what I see and feel how I feel. Although she is sometimes in two minds about whether to set out, she's always glad she's done it by the time we return home.
"See!" I say, "I told you you'd enjoy it. Do you want to come out tomorrow?"
"Maybe."
And that's the way it goes: always dipping her toe but never willing to take the plunge.

I think, although your partner (or, indeed the rest of your family) might come to understand your passion, there's every chance that they will not live it in the way you do. This is not an entirely bad thing in our house – we haven't got room for any more bikes, for a start.

25. WATCHING CYCLING

Pro cycling is not just on the telly: sometimes it comes to your street! Part of the magic of a sport where you can follow in the footsteps (ride in the tyre prints?) of the greats is that the moveable feast also sometimes comes to your neighbourhood. Shelly loves a bit of live cycling and generally gets more excited than I do. We've had the great good fortune to have the Tour of Britain literally pass by our door on one occasion and within ten miles of the house on two more. In 2019, we also got a stage depart in my hometown of Altrincham, which meant a fantastic opportunity to get up close and personal (this is not stalking!) with the riders in a way that you never can with other sportsmen in other sports. Added to that, we've seen the Tour de France three times and, of course, I went on a very, very damp trip to see the World Championships in Harrogate.

Travelling out to see a stage on the roadside needs perfect planning, but you should also be prepared to be flexible. In 2013, Shelly and I travelled to Paris to see the final stage of the Tour. We were very fortunate to get a hotel just off the Champs Élysées and the plan was to get the Metro over to Versailles in the morning to see the riders depart, and then head back to the Champs to find a place to watch the grand finale. Everything was decided – we had even bought our train tickets the day before, so we knew we'd have little waiting time.

After breakfast, we left the hotel at 10am and were headed for our station when I saw that the crowds were still very thin on the Champs, and there was a gap by the railings just up from the finish line. Change of plans. We spent the following ten hours in that gap, watching the boulevard fill up, and were kept going by the sense of anticipation, a couple of filled baguettes (I cannot remember the fillings, sorry) and lots of bottles of water. There were plenty of interesting things to see to punctuate the waiting hours in the July sun: many former champions were milling about as it was the Tour's 100th edition. (I managed to get Sean Kelly's autograph, but Eddy Merckx skilfully avoided me.)

When, at long last, the peloton arrived in Paris and came storming by, flying over those cobbles en masse like a train on a track, it was a moment I shall never forget. The great thing about this final stage is that they didn't just go by the once, and we got to see them again and again as they raced up to the Arc de Triomphe and back down the hill, passing us once more on the far side of the road. It truly was value for money, and our seats were free!

It is generally the case, though, when watching a Tour stage, that much time and energy is spent for very little actual spectating. In 2014, we travelled across to The Strines (yes, that Strines), just west of Sheffield, as the Tour de France paid a visit to Yorkshire. Up and out early, we arrived, as we had done in Paris, when there were still very few others there, and were quite chuffed that we had managed to park the car so close to the action. It required a walk of less than half an hour to claim our spot! Again, it was hours before the first signs of the Tour arrived with the police outriders, and then the publicity caravan. And then another gap before the tv helicopters appeared over the crest across the valley, and, finally, we saw the riders. Knowing the road as I did had me choose our position wisely and, from where we were, we were able to watch the peloton stream over the top and down the steep Ewden Bank in a thin line before they disappeared into the trees below us. They then faced the almost equally steep climb up out of the trough past where we were standing. The narrow road and sudden incline had a concertina effect which saw the peloton slow considerably, giving us fantastic views of the riders at close quarters as they went by.

And then they were gone.

And so we packed up our things to walk back to the car. The crowded road meant it took us considerably longer to get back and, when we did, we were stuck in an immediate traffic jam. I realised later that three roads from different viewing positions all converged at the same point. This meant slow going. Very slow. It took us four hours to travel just under six miles back to the junction with the main road. So slow was it, in fact, that Shelly was able to get out of the car and go to the ladies' at the Strines Inn, and buy us some crisps at the bar, without me having to pull out of the line of traffic to wait for her.

Sometimes, even parking miles away doesn't work to your advantage. Our trip to Ventoux in 2016 wasn't all about me riding up it. Three days following my ascent, the Tour went up but, by the time their stage came around, the weather had taken a turn for the worse, and high winds meant that the stage finish was brought down from the summit to Chalet Reynard.

As we left the car at the foot of the mountain just outside Sault, the sun was still shining, but it was a good deal colder than it had been on previous mornings. A mile up the road and I was wishing I hadn't left my coat in the car, but Shelly pointed out – perfectly reasonably at the time – that it was still very early (not yet nine o'clock) and the day was bound to warm up. As with every trip, I had been keen to cover all eventualities, and had been more concerned with running out of water on the mountain. This being the case, I was lugging up five litres. Even though I had a base layer and a long-sleeved winter cycling jersey on, I could still feel the wind cutting through me. It was a ten-mile hike to Chalet Reynard and, as the sun rose and the temperature refused to rise with it, I became more and more concerned. Spirits were still high, though, so I hoped for the best.

Once more, our early arrival led to us snagging a great place to see the race and we were virtually on the finish line. We settled down for the day – we had nearly five hours to wait – but I was struggling more and more with the temperature. The downside of being a racing snake is that I have less body fat to keep me warm. At one point, in a bid to warm up, I went across the road to the restaurant to get a couple of cups of coffee. I was so cold that I couldn't get my hands to work; they would not tear the sugar sachets or pick up one of those pointless little stirrers. It greatly amused the gentleman selling me the coffee until it came to the point where he expected me to get money out of my pocket. Then, he had to wait, stern-faced, as I failed at least three times to grip my euros. In the end, I was so cold that I gladly went back to the restaurant to pay €100 for a cycling jacket I knew I would probably never need again. This made some difference. Not much, but enough. (I do use it quite often, in fact. It is highly windproof and, importantly, has detachable sleeves and so it has become my go-to gilet.)

History will tell you that this was the stage where Chris Froome left his bike and started running up the road. We were relayed this news by a lovely French lady next to us but were convinced she'd missed something in translation. (She kept exclaiming, "Froome running!" which we thought at the time just had to be wrong.) We got a great photo of Thomas De Gendt crossing the line and then, a few minutes later, the Sky boys riding in looking less than pleased with their day's work. It wasn't until we saw the race replayed on Eurosport later that night that we realised she'd been spot on.

Following the end of the race, our section of crowd was penned in* while the team buses, which had all been parked on the Sault road (and thus our way down) were moved. By now, I was not the only one having problems with the temperature and, after an or so hour of waiting, the crowd grew restless and began chanting to be let out. Eventually the police gave in and we all filtered down the mountainside. By now, Shelly had started to have problems, too, probably brought on by our hour of immobility, and we were both finding it hard work walking downhill. Cars and campervans were beginning to stream past and so, more in hope than expectation, we began to put our thumbs out to hitch a ride down to Sault. We'd gone on for perhaps another hour and three miles when a campervan actually stopped. We both jumped in with copious "Mercis!" The two guys stared at us as though we were nuts, dressed the way we were on a freezing mountain, but we didn't care as we were both so happy (probably deliriously so) to be onboard. We just sat there, grinning, shaking, and repeating the odd "merci!" until they dropped us off at the car. It was a rather pleasant, warm evening down in Sault.

[*There's always an excited "Look! There I am!" moment when you see yourself on television. Unfortunately, my moment came when I was not in the best of moods, and I can be spotted, squeezed in amongst the throng, frozen and looking decidedly pissed off. Still, fame, though, eh?]

It's not all near-death experiences, though. When the Tour of Britain came within riding distance in 2014, I was doubly fortunate because the stage was on a Monday, which was my day off, so I decided to take it in as part of my ride that day. I chose to watch the race at the closest point the tour came to home, a little climb at a place called Acton Bridge, a village just outside Northwich and an easy 12-mile ride away. My timing was spot on, so spot on, in fact, that I managed to join the course just after the police outriders had gone through, but still a good ten minutes in front of the peloton. As I crossed the bridge*, everyone at roadside started clapping and photographers sitting at the right turn at the base of the climb began snapping away. A moment's confusion turned into joy as it hit me that I'd been mistaken for a lone escapee. As I rounded the bend, I raised my arms to the heavens in triumph. Sadly, my moment of mock victory broke the spell, and there was a collective tut of disgruntlement as everyone suddenly realised that I was just a dickhead on a bike.

This was not the end of my day of fun: once the peloton had passed, most making short work of the short climb, I remounted and followed the route, imploring any and all who were still out and about – and there were quite a few – "Has anybody seen a big bunch of cyclists???" Wonderfully, everybody very helpfully pointed me in the right direction until I eventually turned off the route to make my way back home. (I reckon I could've won that stage had I not had to get back to get lunch on.)

[*Yes, there is a bridge at Acton Bridge, although I don't know what it's called.]

The big take away from our experience of watching live cycling is that it is generally a bloody long day and, much like the Twix adverts from yore, the event itself is over remarkably quickly. As my neighbour, Julie, remarked when we took her to see the Tour of Britain depart in Altrincham: "Was that it???"

Watching live cycling is as much about the occasion and the anticipation of the race as the event itself. Remember, Altrincham was a start, and not just a point on the route, where towns and villages across Europe and the World* will plan and look forward for months to get, if they're lucky, perhaps ten minutes of action. The actual sport is so fleeting, but this doesn't quell the appetite, and there's always excitement and bunting and flags and roadside parties. The Dutch in the rain at the Harrogate World Championships. Belgian flags and the kids (sometimes, not just the kids) running across fields in Flanders to catch the riders a second time. Those campervans perched on the top of Ventoux for a week. Dutch (them again) Corner on Alpe D'Huez. Beefeater Bend on the Galibier in 2019.

Watching cycling on the television is great – I love it: you get to see all that scenery and don't miss a beat of the action – but there's nothing quite like being roadside when the pros fly past. If you get the chance, do it. But take a coat!

[*Perhaps not in the Gulf States, where camels seldom have to push to the front to get a view.]

26. DO YOU HAVE TO STOP PEDALLING WHEN YOU FART?

I've never understood why 'bodily functions' is such a taboo subject. Even that phrase is a euphemism to gloss over the perceived dirtiness. Excretion is as natural and essential to our lives as breathing and, if you are eating a healthy diet, you will likely be pumping out a healthy amount of gas. I fart a lot, and so the question of whether one has to stop pedalling to do it is one that occurred to me early on in my cycling life and continues to be a subject of contemplation.

It's a difficult one. You can be zipping along at a good speed and holding a steady cadence when you begin to feel a build up inside and you know that you're going to have to vent the pressure. Worse, you're struggling up a climb and already putting your body through a great deal of stress. The compulsion is to stop what you are doing to stand up on the pedals a little bit and create some room, but this would lead to a loss in momentum.

There's also that nagging doubt that perhaps it is not actually what you think and might be something far more catastrophic, which puts you in a more tentative frame of mind.

What should you do?

Should you stop pedalling, even if it is just for a second?

In all areas, I believe that it pays to get advice from those who know best, so who better to consult than Colin Sturgess, former pro road rider and winner of National and World Individual Pursuit titles on the track*?

Colin went above and beyond the call of duty for me in going out and performing a special test run. The results were in: did he have to stop pedalling to fart?

"No." he said, "Lift cheek [he's biased towards the left, apparently] slightly off the saddle and toot away."

It has to be remembered that Colin is a seasoned cyclist, with many years riding at the top level. I, too, can ride through a fart, but it takes much practice and confidence in one's own technique. I still cannot do a track stand, though. I don't think that the two are linked. And, on that note…

[*and, it goes without saying, top bloke.]

27. AGAIN, WHY?

There's obviously a huge physical side to be enjoyed from riding a bike, but the mental side of things is extremely important too. Let's face it, if we wanted to use cycling merely to get fit, we need never leave the house. We could sit on our turbo trainers, in a nice, dry environment, with tv and/or music, and the constant availability of a proper loo should the need arise. Indeed, there are plenty of people who will do this if they go to spinning classes as part of their fitness regime, but then never venture out on the roads on two wheels.

As I pointed out in an earlier chapter, for me, the indoor bit is of use simply to make the outdoor bit more enjoyable. Inside, I am training – on the road, I am cycling. Even if it's a bloody hard ride, even if I have targeted a local hill to get a PB on, I have never viewed my road cycling as training. There will be some (possibly many) who say that you have to train on the road, but the problem for me is that it's all too easy for every ride to then become nothing more than a training session, and then you risk losing the magic. I stopped cycling with one group because every ride turned into a chain gang: head down and ride flat out. Okay, there was good banter beforehand and I was undoubtedly getting fitter, but I can't say that I actually enjoyed many of those rides.

The magic of cycling is that it can take you away from real life. It takes you back to those times when you were off exploring as a kid. It takes you out of the hustle, bustle and stress of the town and city and into the countryside. You could do this by running, but it takes far longer to get where you're going, you can't see what's going on over high hedgerows and, if you stop for a rest, you actually stop. Stop pedalling on a bike and you'll generally keep moving (unless you're going uphill, obviously, but, even then, you will move, just not in the direction you want to). You could do it by car, but then you're still stuck with motoring stress and, as you're in the car, you're not outside. You could do it on a motorbike – and I see plenty of weekend bikers out on country roads – but you'd be going far too fast to appreciate your environment and, at the end, where's the sense of achievement?

I've started rides grumbling about something or other: I've left the house on the back of an argument with Shelly (I was right, obviously), or I've got on my bike following yet another depressingly bad day at work. Within moments, all the emotions I had simply melted away in the act of riding my bike. All thoughts are turned to the road, to the act of cycling and cycling alone. Shelly has asked me what I think about when I ride, and my answer is always "Nothing". She can't comprehend this as something is amiss in her world if there is nothing to stress about. If she is not worrying, she finds it worrying.
"How can you think of nothing?"
I don't think of nothing, I just don't think. Obviously, my mind does not become some sort of vacuum, void or black hole – there is still stuff going on inside there – but all things that are

going on outside of my immediate experience, all things past and future, are pushed into the background. Whilst cycling, everything is an instant snapshot of the present:

Hill.
Pothole.
View!
Argh, headwind.
Lorry too close (arsehole).
Cows! Hard hill (bugger).
Another view!
Weeeeeee! down the other side!
Horsey! (I have to say hello to horses, either with a clicking sound or by saying "hello" (it's good manners). On solo rides, if they are close to the road, I'll stop for a chat and to feed and stroke them, making sure the bike is out of reach as they seem to like chewing the brake hoods. This is another thing that makes me happy.)

There are always brief negatives that punctuate the route, those that usually have four wheels and an engine, but these are quickly forgotten. Some instances stay with me and colour the rest of the ride. I've stopped to help baby thrushes, mice and voles off the road, had a buzzard lift off a gate post and fly alongside at head height a few feet away for a while, spotted numerous weasels streak across quiet country lanes as they hear me coming, and once, wonderfully, I had a peregrine falcon swoop down in front of me and lead me down a road for a few hundred yards. I accelerated to a sprint to hang onto its tail but, although I am "The Flying Goat of Leafy

Cheshire", I couldn't quite catch it. It ended the chase by lifting up into a tree to watch me go by. I spent the rest of the ride buzzing with the experience.

Sometimes, thoughts do drift in – some have been quite profound, some funny, some managed to be so fortunate as to make it into this book – but most of them are quickly banished as I round the next corner and return to the now. It'd be great to have all my genius moments whilst on the bike. As it is, they tend to come in the bath (Eureka!) or just as I'm dropping off at night. Bath stuff I can usually remember, even if the convoluted stream of consciousness gets a little lost. Night-time thoughts can get easily forgotten once sleep takes me, so I had the cunning idea of putting a pen and pad by the bed, so that I could jot ideas down in the dark and, come the dawn, they would be there for me to see. Unfortunately, my nocturnal musings are usually so illegible I sit there in the morning, thinking "What the bloody hell have I written there???"

Even when in a group, cycling can be a wholly internal experience. Riding up a stiff hill, all talking gradually ceases as everyone recedes into their own private struggle with gravity, sound is distilled to heavy, rhythmic breathing (and the annoying creak from your mate's bottom bracket). Your heartbeat fills your head and the yard or so of road ahead fills your vision. Here, too, are snapshots. I remember, very clearly, on one hill, gazing down past my pedal and noting

"Oh, a bird's leg!" as I struggled oh-so-very-slowly onward. (Cycling can be hugely uplifting. The one constant downer is the amount of roadkill we get to see at close quarters.) Occasionally, you'll look up to see where the end is, which is usually further than you'd thought it would be, but then it's back to your own battle. Nothing else, in that protracted moment, matters. The act of cycling takes over everything.

Cycling transports you, very obviously, physically, but it is its ability to psychologically transport you that can be massively beneficial. It is the very antithesis of lying in bed at three in the morning, staring at the ceiling, with every single worry in your life dancing around your head. Get on a bike and all ills are left at home. Of course, they're still there for when you get back but, for the amount of time you're in the saddle, they just aren't important.

THIS IS IMPORTANT: CYCLING TAKES YOU ON A HOLIDAY FROM YOUR BRAIN!

And when you get back, you're usually in such a bloody good mood that, well, were they ever so bad after all? You might have had the toughest, coldest, wettest ride and you'll be exhausted but you'll also be in a better mental place. This is the magic.

When I return from a ride, I am, I'm frequently informed, annoyingly upbeat. This is not my fault, of course, as it's due to all the endorphins triggered by the cycling. Endorphins are released as a response to pain, stress and also fear so:

The Theory of Cycling Relativity: Law 25
The harder your ride has been, the happier you should feel at the end of it, especially if you have had a near-death event!

I am aware that my own personal buoyancy is exaggerated because Shelly has usually spent the time I was riding engaging in acts of drudgery and so our mood contrast is, perhaps, starker. It is sad that my happiness does not seem to rub off, especially when I haven't noticed just how clean the kitchen floor is. She, too, could be as happy as I: she just needs to ride more! I'm more than happy to lend a hand with the cleaning but, apparently, my 'clean' is different from Shelly's 'clean'. Even when I broke my wrist and had carried on in pain through sub-zero temperatures for an hour (like a dickhead, I know), my mood was only mildly dampened by the fact that I knew I'd done some sort of damage to myself which would undoubtedly lead to time off the bike.

Because you know that cycling makes you happy, you want to do it more, which makes you fitter, so you can do it more, which makes you happy. It's a wonderful, spoked, virtuous circle. There is a risk, as is often pointed out to me here at home, that you come to rely on cycling for all your highs, but fear not, that's where coffee comes in!

MOTIVATION

Even though there's nothing that cannot be made better by a bike ride, sometimes it's difficult to get yourself up and out. Dark, cold, wet or windy days it's easy to think, "Maybe tomorrow". Certain days, whatever the weather, you'd rather just sit and watch the television.

Everyone has different motivations. For many, the simple act of cycling is enough, and choosing only to ride on the odd sunny, wind-free day presents no motivational issues. Others need a target, and a sportive or a date with a large mountain can provide a focus and the impetus to get out and ride when sometimes they'd rather not.

Analysing myself, it seems to be that motivation is circular: my mental side has a duty of care for my physical side and, if my physical state is in a better place, then so is my mental state. I love riding my bike, so it follows that cycling time is happy time. I appreciate that, however I'm feeling sitting around the house, I will feel infinitely better ten minutes into a ride, even if it's raining.

There's a positive/negative angle to my approach. So, as much as I'm aware that I will feel good if I go on a ride, I also know that I will be plagued with guilt if I miss the chance. (I do get, so I'm reliably informed, a little grumpy if I don't take the chance to go and ride.) The knowledge that riding will keep up my physical fitness and mental wellbeing is coupled with the fear of loss of fitness that not riding will bring, and I'm well aware that, the older I get, I have to work harder to keep that fitness. I think that, in fact, I probably train to be a little bit better than I need to be.

Is it silly? If I was less fit, I would still cycle, and I would still enjoy the rides as much. I would perhaps not go as far, and may well go everywhere that much more slowly, but I would be happy. I suppose that it's the knowing that I am better than I was – that feeling of achievement – that gives me a mental boost that spills over into my other life as a biped. Obviously, the flipside of this is the fear of fitness loss and the knowledge that the day will come that I might not be able to ride up that hill.

It's this fear of fitness loss that puts me on the turbo trainer when the weather outside is awful. I get no psychological kicks from indoor training, other than the pat on the back I can give myself for completing a hard session and the understanding that this will make riding outside a better experience. There is no joy to be had for me on a turbo trainer – all the joy is out on the road. This is why I went out on an icy day in January only to break my wrist, and this is why I kept riding on that day for as long as I could before being driven home by pain and cold. Sometimes, it's harder for me not to ride. Am I addicted to cycling? Possibly, but there are worse things to be addicted to.

I have now just passed fifty, and I'm fitter, leaner and lighter than I was at twenty-five, although, sadly, my hair didn't quite manage to make the journey with me. I fully expect to have a longer life than I did back then, not just because of the physical aspects, but because I have a system in place that can immediately take care of all my stress.

I'm a happy dude!

July 11th 2016
7.20am
Shelly takes a photo of a slightly nervous me making my final preparations before I swing my leg over, start the Garmin (if it ain't on Strava…) and spin out of the car park to begin the ride.

The plan is to save as much energy as I can for as long as I can, so I take the initial 6km to the bend at Saint-Estève at a ridiculously easy pace (I imagine that I am pedalling on eggshells I'm trying not to break). Even so, I worry, as I am still passing the few others beginning their ascent at this early hour. There are some, like me, clothed in summer lycra; and some who've seemingly come more dressed for the Alps in winter. I hope they're wrong.

About three kilometres in, I overtake a guy on a recumbent bike riding with two mates. I wish them good morning and good luck. Again, I'm a little perturbed by the speed at which I drop them – "Am I going too fast???" – but I feel comfortable and so hold my pace.

The roadside is already littered with campervans and we're only just out of Bédoin. Gradually, the gradient increases until, here we are: Saint-Estève and that famous (infamous?) left-hand bend that heralds the forest and the climb proper. I swing the bike around and, as the front end goes up, click down into my easiest gear, safe in the knowledge that this is where I'll be for the rest of the ascent. That early ramp does not seem as vicious as I'd imagined it might be and so I settle into a rhythm I think I can hold for the long term.

The campervans are parked up in every nook and cranny between road and trees and the assembled Tour fans are just beginning to awake. It is not long at all before my approach is noticed. I watch as a family up ahead are just sitting down to breakfast. The father spies me first, and then, like a group of meerkats, the whole group is up and looking at me intently as I spin up to their patch.

"C'est le Maillot à Pois Rouges!" exclaims the father, pointing.

'Here we go', I think, as I prepare myself for a bit of abuse, but it doesn't come.

"Allez! Allez! Courage mon ami!" he shouts. All around the table are up and cheering. I do a fist pump and grin my appreciation. A little bit further up the road, another family look down to see what all the fuss is about, and I receive the same welcome. It's quite amazing. It also means that there's nowhere to hide and, as I grind my way up beneath the wooden canopy, I know that there's no way on earth I can put a foot down.

Every van I pass, I get cheered. I try to reply to their encouragement, but talking is not easy and so it's kept to a very brief "Bonjour. Oui – allez!" or just "Merci". The conversations with English fans are very short indeed. They're easily spotted, with their vans bedecked in Union Jacks. As I pass, they shout "Froomey!", and I shout "Froomey!" back at them. Simple, but effective.

It's tough but manageable. At home, I've ridden eight, nine, ten percent climbs and I know I can do it, but those hills are usually no more than two kilometres and I'm normally completely knackered when I get to the top. Here, I am staring down (or up) the barrel of that gradient for the next ten kilometres, and then there's more to come once I'm out of the forest! Fortunately, the lack of hairpins and the fact that there's very little change in gradient means that I can hold my steady cadence, tapping it out to the rhythm of my breathing. Mentally, it's hard going – one 100 metre stretch of wooded road is exactly the same as the next and so there are no views to take my mind off the task in hand – until I realise one thing: back at the turn, I hadn't actually dropped into my easiest gear! I still have room to spare! I am roughly halfway through the forest when I discover this, and it brings me to an immediate and remarkable realisation. I am more than up to the job I've set myself, and all the feelings of anxiety that have plagued me during the six months since I'd booked the trip fade away to be replaced by an unshakeable confidence and even a sense of euphoria. This is not the ogre that I had built up in my mind: I know I can do this. This, added to the continued support from the roadside, lifts me through the rest of the forest. I'm finding this ride less arduous than the Montagne De Lure – even the flies here aren't as bad.

To paraphrase Edmund Hillary, I am going to knock this bastard off!

I pass a Belgian pair, one of whom has the same bike as me. I comment on it as I ride around them, but get no answer. Ah, well. As I think I'm nearing the end of the treeline – it turns out to be a mere clearing, offering a glimpse of my red and white finishing line – I am passed by a young girl wearing a Durham University jersey. I begin to quicken my pace slightly, intending to have a chat, but I notice that the column of flies she is towing up is massive; far bigger, I think, than my own. I'm not sure I want to combine the two, so I sit back and return to my own pace, content to let her go.

Then, the road starts to flatten, and I see sunlight once again. I pass the road up from Sault, joining on my right and then, all of a sudden, I'm at Chalet Reynard. As planned, Shelly is waiting by the café with spare water, and is standing, arm out, like a proper swanny, but I don't need it. Much as I am impressed with her, I can't stop, so I give her a winning smile, sweep straight past and climb out of the saddle to hit the bend and the steep gradient that follows as the road arcs round to the left.

As I rise to the top of that stretch, I have my breath taken away as I'm presented with the glorious panorama that is Provence, laid out like a map, almost a mile below me. What the forest had kept hidden from me is all the more majestic for its sudden appearance. (It's like walking up the steps to Montmartre's Sacré-Coeur without looking back and then turning at the top to see all of Paris spread before you, but ten times better.)

Now, I have this wonderful vista to my left, and the bait that is the tower at the summit in front of me. Shelly passes me in the car as she goes up to find a place for "THE PHOTO" (she has her instructions!) and the road is still lined, wherever possible with campervans. I am just counting down to the finish, now, and look forward to each of the kilometre posts. I am being driven on by sheer euphoria, especially when, expecting to see the four to go mark, I arrive at the 3km post (I must have missed one while I was sightseeing). Every time the road takes me around one more headland, I'm one headland closer, and that bloody tower is looming.

I pass a guy in a kilt playing the bagpipes: bizarre.

Emotion starts to get the better of me as I approach the Simpson Memorial. I cannot stop, though, and will pay my respects on the way down, so I tip Tom a salute and sprint by. There's Shelly with the camera, so I get out of the saddle for the money shot, and then I'm back down to finish the job. She nips by again in the car, "You're nearly there!"

Don't I bloody know it!

And then, one hour forty minutes after I left Bédoin, I swing sharp right and up the final ramp to the top.

And I am there.

It hit me whilst sitting at the summit at 9am on that glorious Provençale morning. This was the culmination of everything that had begun with that first time back on my bike seven years before, and the fulfilment of a dream forged by all the Tour de France battles I had watched play out, not just on these slopes, but on every Alp and Pyrenean col. I had lived the dream! I was as happy and, at the same time, calm, as I have ever been. I was serene. I'd had my Cingles card stamped as proof of my ascent, but I now didn't feel the need to go back down and do it twice more: I knew I could, but I would never beat this feeling, so what would be the point? I had my photo taken by that famous summit signpost, and then I sat for a while, alone (Shelly had popped into the souvenir shop to buy a little polka-dotted lead cyclist to mark the occasion), gazing down at the world below through the morning haze and drank it all in, before setting off back down to Sault for some breakfast. But I could happily have stayed there all day.

This, I thought at the time.

This is why.

ACKNOWLEDGEMENTS

Obviously, I have to first and foremost thank my wife Shelly, who puts up with what is something of an obsession with (for the most part) patience and good humour. I should have the words, "Well, okay, but don't be all day!" tattooed across my heart.

Then, chronologically, thanks to my brother Simon, without whom I'd never have had my series of second-hand bikes nor someone to try and keep up with when I was a nipper.

My mate Paul, who inadvertently rekindled my love for the bike by cajoling me into joining him on that sportive all those years ago.

Al at Polocini, who set me up to meet the guys I ride with now: Ken, Col, Andy, Lee and Ged, along with a few other random souls who coalesce most weekends for a few hours of riding our side of the Pennines and around Leafy Cheshire. I guess no one else would have me.

And thanks to four chaps for the help I received in the writing and producing of this book. Simon Warren and Colin Sturgess very kindly donated their time and energy in very different ways, and Ken Matheson and Gareth Cartman let me pick their brains when I needed to. I originally met all four through Twitter, which has been, over the years, a medium that has allowed me to cross paths with a number of cycling journalists such as Daniel Friebe, Ed Pickering, Jeremy Whittle and Peter Stuart who, while commissioning editor at Cyclist magazine, published a couple of my articles and showed me that I wasn't just messing about at this writing lark.

Funny to think that all this began with a 140-character limit.

Printed in Great Britain
by Amazon